Laughing Together

The Value of Humor
in Family Life

Dotsey Welliver

BRETHREN PRESS
Elgin, Illinois

Laughing Together: The Value of Humor in Family Life

BRETHREN PRESS, 1451 Dundee Avenue, Elgin, IL 60120.

Cover design by Kathy Kline
Edited by Leslie Keylock

Unless otherwise noted, scriptural quotations are from the New International Version, © 1978 New York International Bible Society. Used with permission.

Library of Congress Cataloging in Publication Data

Welliver, Dotsey.
  Laughing together.

  Bibliography: p.
  1. Family—Religious life.   2. Laughter—Religious aspects—Christianity.   I. Title.
BV4526.2.W45   1986   241'.4   84-12890
  ISBN 0-87178-226-X

Manufactured in the United States of America

For My Larger Family—

All The Saints

Of My Local Church Fellowship.

They Make Me Laugh.

The author wishes to thank Glenn F. Arnold and P. Mark Fackler of the Wheaton College Graduate School who graciously read through and critiqued early versions of the manuscript.

Contents

Preface

One Sunday morning I was standing in the foyer of a typical Protestant church with sincere, likeable Christians saying rather mundane things, when an unbidden thought suddenly struck me as being very funny. I threw back my head and howled, as I am wont to do on occasion.

A dear, well-meaning sister stepped up to me a few moments later and began a conversation. As I recall, her advice went something like this: "Dotsey, you sure do like to laugh and jest a lot. Something I read in the Bible recently bothered me and I just have to share it with you. In Matthew 12:36 Jesus says we will have to give account on the day of judgment for every careless and idle word we have spoken. Also in Matthew 5:37, he says our 'yes' should simply be 'yes,' and our 'no' be 'no.' I hope you won't take what I'm saying in the wrong way. I know you mean well. But I think the Bible disapproves of your lack of seriousness."

I rose heroically to the occasion and thanked my friend for her interest in my spiritual welfare. I then went home to do some serious soul searching.

Could I be wrong in feeling that my sense of humor was perfectly harmless? Was there truly something unspiritual about me that caused me to love to laugh and jest? Was the Enemy approaching me through my use of so many "idle" words? Could I live through even one day saying simply "yes" or "no"? Was that what Jesus truly meant? I doubted it.

I let my mind do a flashback to the days when I was growing up. I do not think that as a child I was particularly known for being the effervescent, merry type. Since I loved to read, much of my time was spent in quiet pursuits. As a sharecropper's daughter, I also spent long hours working in the cotton fields.

My quiet world was nevertheless filled with delightful, chuckle-producing sights. I thought that God had my own welfare in mind when he created so many fascinating and amusing things. To me, the "woolly" worms on the old sycamore tree were funny. The lanky-legged spiders scooting up and down the cotton plants were funny. An ancient farm wagon, fat sides bursting out with its gorge of cotton, bumping and squeaking its way home on arthritic wheels in the evanescent light of sunset was somehow both holy and hilarious. I laughed at the gabby chickens when I went to feed them and they squawked and pecked at my bare toes. Watching squealing, newborn pigs wrestling for a feeding place at their banquet table was funnier than a ringside seat at the circus.

But best by far were all the funny words in the world. How marvelous that God would actually allow his truth to be expressed in human ideas and words, many of them full of wonder, joy, delight, and amusement. Some words were simply funny by sound, apart from their images. I loved to say my favorite words over and over again, and laugh hilariously at the funny sounds that came out of my mouth.

x

Sometimes Daddy and I would experiment with nonsense verses, and again I would peal with laughter. I made up puns and wrote some absolutely horrible humorous poems. I committed to memory many of the funny country expressions and stories I learned as I was growing up.

And books were a world of entertainment and laughter all their own. I remember being sprawled all over our faded old couch one afternoon reading a book, when I suddenly heehawed. I chortled, howled, hooted, screeched, gasped, and otherwise guffawed my way through several more pages until tears ran down my cheeks.

This was too much, even for my dry-witted father. He walked through, glanced around to see what I was laughing at, and then snorted on his way out, "No book could possibly be that funny." But Mark Twain's essay on curing a cold *was* that funny. Even funnier. I read it three or four times.

A decade rolled around. I married. Then funny babies started arriving at my house. I laughed at them and they laughed at me. In fact, they laughed at almost everything, and I laughed with them. Along with the daily dose of challenge, experiment, admonishment, and even irritation went a healthy spoonful of enjoyment and delight at the smallest and wackiest sorts of things.

I laughed with toddlers and kindergartners. I laughed with lisping first-graders when their front teeth were out. I laughed with long-limbed adolescents and teenaged men-children. We helped shape each other's egos to manageable proportions with our bantering.

Even today I laughed with my last funny baby (now twelve) as we delighted in the antics of our kitten romping around in the first snow of his life.

I cannot seem to give up the habit.

Had I been displeasing God all those years? In creation, when God pronounced all the things he had made good, did that not include the mechanism he built into the human being for laughter?

Would it not have included, furthermore, the potential God gave us for self-awareness – our ability to comprehend our own shortcomings and the incongruities in the world around us – and our ability to make jokes about them?

Because of the incident at church I began to do some serious research into the topics of laughter and humor. During the research I shared some of my thoughts (particularly concerning the use of humor in our families) with women at retreats and various other speaking engagements. I was surprised at the number who came to me later and stressed the need for such emphasis. There was no question that many others felt the way I did. The majority opinion indicated that, in our tension-laden society, more relaxed and healthy laughter is needed, especially in our homes.

As a part of my own developing philosophy of humor, I have come to believe we should encourage wholesome laughter. We need not be afraid to use it simply because it can be misused. Laughter is God's gift and needs no further justification. It is vital to our welfare physically, mentally, emotionally, and, yes, spiritually. Laughter is an attribute that can help sustain us through the barren deserts in life. It can also heighten our enjoyment of the sweet meadow places. A humorous perspective can lighten the load of our daily work and help us transcend some of our trials. It certainly can help us enrich our family lives.

Some of the results of my reflection appear in this book. I laughed heartily during much of the research, though I admit that the parts that show the brokenness of the human race and the abuse of God's gift were depressing. I laughed through many of the pages even as I typed the manuscript. I just cannot seem to break the habit.

Would you like to hazard a guess as to what we will do first when we step through the gates of heaven? Singers, of course, plan to burst into song. Artists will want to paint a picture capturing the splendor of the celestial city. I strongly suspect engineers will want to study the golden bridges spanning the River of Life, and architects will want to inspect the heavenly mansions.

But as for me, I expect to laugh. I cannot think of a more wonderful and heartening truth than that I should make heaven. All because of God's free forgiveness and grace.

Yes, I plan to laugh. And laugh and laugh. It's an awfully hard habit to break.

1

Understanding Humor:
A Painless Dissection

*"There is a time for everything. . . . A time to
weep, and a time to laugh"* (Eccl. 3:1,4).

During the Civil War, two Quaker ladies were
discussing the possible victor. The first lady said,
"I think Mr. Davis's side will win."

"But why," the other asked, "dost thee think
so?"

"Because," replied the first lady, "Mr. Davis is a
praying man."

"True," agreed the second, "but so is Mr. Lincoln."

"Oh, I know he is," came the reply, "but the
Lord will think Mr. Lincoln is only joking."

The Quaker lady does not stand alone in looking
askance at the idea of joking. The Puritans and
earlier religious groups also questioned the value
of humor. As early as A.D. 390 Chrysostom had
preached that the world is not a theater in which to
laugh and that it is "not God who gives us the
chance to play, but the devil" (Hyers 1981, 15).

Humor has been attacked, discussed, analyzed, and defended for centuries. One may wonder if anything else can be said that would really matter. I believe it can.

Let's take a look.

Essayist E. B. White once said, "Humor can be dissected, as a frog can, but the thing dies in the process."

Now I don't want to kill a "frog." In fact, I want to help us understand and enjoy the creature. We can learn a lot by taking a good look at it from different angles. A bit of background on humor may be helpful before we start thinking about the main subject, improving our family life through the use of humor.

God has given hearty laughter to his children as a special gift. A puppy can wag his tail to express happiness. Primate laughter has been documented in chimpanzees by anthropologist Jane Goodall. Apes are said to use a form of laughter to signal playfulness. Experimental studies have shown that the higher primates produce something akin to laughter—facial movements, interruptions of normal breathing patterns, and general muscular movements (Cross and Cross 16).

Monkeys in zoos sometimes seem to demonstrate a sense of humor by squirting water or throwing dirt at passersby and then making the facial contortions of laughter.

However, no one has yet ever heard an animal rear back, hold both sides, and let go with a loud belly laugh. Certainly, no one has ever heard a beast tell a joke.

Essentially, laughter is a human function.

The English essayist, William Hazlitt, writing in the nineteenth century, once observed that man is the only being that both laughs and weeps, because he is the only one conscious of the difference between what things are and what they really ought to be.

Humor can trigger a glimpse of the gap between the estranged sinful self and the self God intends us to be. The inconsistency between who we really are and who we ought to be is often seen through humor (Parrott 21).

Do we really fully appreciate the gift of laughter? It is, after speech, one of the main ways we communicate with each other. Laughter knows no particular religion, politics, or age group.

Laughter can be used for God's glory. When we laugh we affirm God's good gift of humor.

And it doesn't really matter if we're a little child or a senior citizen, we smile and we laugh. The scholar and the simpleton both laugh. People in Austria and people in Australia enjoy the amusing things that happen to us all. Laughter is a sign of spontaneity, health, warmth, and happiness.

Laughter is like a personal monogram. I remember one day hearing someone in another room laugh. By his laugh I knew instantly who was in that room.

Laughter has many rhythms as well as tones. We not only have unique lifestyles; we also have special laugh-styles. A great variety of combinations is possible. Paul, the executive, may indulge in a discreet chuckle. I may burst out in a jubilant shout, a hearty heehaw, or a leonine roar. You may emit a smile, a simper, a snicker, a smirk, or a shriek. Surely this is a testament to the mind-boggling creativity God built into his world.

Mood also imposes its patterns. Think of the image that comes into your mind when you think of merry laughter, a silly giggle, a weird cackle, a mocking howl, or a jeering guffaw.

Laughter is communication. It can convey pleasure or embarrassment, friendliness or derision.

One sign of "humanness" we look for in a very young baby is that first smile (Hyers 1960, 216). I think of the time a friend came over with her husband and their wee firstborn. The baby broke into a grin when I tickled her under the chin. The inability to smile can indicate emotional starvation and mental problems in children, in fact.

What exactly is humor? Lots of answers have

been given, but one of the best is that of the Canadian humorist, Stephen Leacock. He called it the "kindly contemplation of the incongruities of life."

Philosopher John Morreall of Northwestern University (1983) says humor is a sudden pleasant psychological shift. Others have defined it as an inward attitude of playfulness and suggest that laughter is its accompanying sound effect.

However, humor can be shown in other ways than outright laughter. A quiet chuckle, a smile, even a merry twinkle of the eye or an "I-give-up" expression on the face can indicate that something funny has happened.

Humor in its essence is an inward frame of mind, a flexible way of experiencing life. How's this for a broad definition of humor?: "Any communication perceived as amusing, bringing about laughter, smiles, or a general feeling of merriment."

Interestingly enough, in its original form, the word *humor* described any of the four fluids (blood, phlegm, black bile, and yellow bile) considered responsible for one's health and disposition (Robinson 9).

Humor is more than a joke. Humor is fun. Humor is approaching life with a merry spirit.

One psychologist, J. Y. T. Grieg, has in the appendix of his book listed eighty-eight separate theories of laughter and comedy.

To aid our understanding here, however (and to avoid that painful surgical incision on our frog), humor specialists rely mostly on four basic categories of humor, each including different variations.

Let's take a short look at each of them.

1. *The incongruity ("surprise") theory.*
Picture this ad from a smalltown Kansas newspaper:

> Young eligible farmer wants to meet marriageable girl with tractor. Please send picture of tractor.

What kind of response does that ad produce in you? Shock? Surprise? Unexpectedness? My mind immediately jumped ahead to a photograph of a beautiful girl. But the next two words erased that picture, and I was left instead with a picture of a tractor—a plain, old, ugly tractor!

Many jokes use that juxtaposition of two incompatible ideas to make us laugh. We are led to think one way, and while we are thinking of a logical way to work the story out, the punch line quickly hits us and we are jolted out of a logical conclusion and into the illogical or unexpected conclusion. How do we respond? We howl with laughter.

That's what the eighteenth-century German philosopher Immanuel Kant observed. Laughter, he wrote, arises "from the sudden transformation of a strained expectation into nothing." We anticipate the next step, but it isn't there, and we fall into laughter.

2. *The superiority ("derision") theory.*
Dr. Ahmad was talking to Les Roberts about the condition of his wife after her yearly examination.

"I'm a little concerned," he said. "I don't like her looks."

"Well," Les replied, "don't worry about that. I've never liked her looks either."

That joke is an example of unexpected derision. The derision theory of humor goes back at least as far as Thomas Hobbes, a seventeenth-century British philosopher. In some forms it goes all the way back to Plato and Aristotle, for that matter. Hobbes defined laughter as a kind of "sudden glory" that we perceive when we observe the infirmities or problems of others and compare them to some "eminency" in ourselves (Goldstein and McGhee 7).

We also chuckle when Bob outstrips his mean competitors, or proud Mary is embarrassed, or Dopey Danny does something really stupid.

This kind of laughter does not always have to be contemptuous or scornful. The laughter of superiority can still be combined with sympathy, congeniality, and even identification and empathy. We can feel sorry for proud Mary even though we may laugh because she got what was coming to her.

The derision theory seems incomplete, though. Anyone who has watched young children at play, for instance, would have to argue that such a theory does not apply to all forms of humor. Children laugh uproariously sometimes over seemingly meaningless things. Their laughter has nothing to do with scorn for their playmates or feelings of superiority over other little children.

Some laughter does contain an unworthy element, though. Laughter has, along with other good gifts, become tainted by sin. I am still convinced, however, that we can laugh over matters incompatible with contempt, scorn, aggression, or feelings of superiority over others.

3. *Relief, release and liberation theories.*

José lives in a small village in a dictatorship. He went to the polls on election day. The voting official handed the unlettered peasant a sealed envelope and showed him where to drop it. Instead, he started to open the envelope.

"What do you think you are doing?" the official shouted. José replied that he simply wanted to know who he was voting for.

"You must be crazy," barked the official. "You know we vote by secret ballot here."

In totalitarian countries such a form of humor is quite often used for release. In a free society, a joke is more often something like an appetizer. It whets our taste and enlivens our enjoyment of life. But in an oppressed nation, jesting is one way people put up with what would otherwise be intolerable situations.

Laughter and prayer are sometimes about the only weapons a prisoner can use against his captor. Political jokes become a safety-valve release and sometimes even a weapon. Such jokes help the prisoner feel free in the only sense available to him.

British philosopher Herbert Spencer suggests that laughter is a discharge mechanism for excess emotional energy (Goldstein and McGee, 11).

Similarly, psychoanalyst Sigmund Freud wrote that comic pleasure is due to an "economy of psychic expenditure." Humor makes an event that would otherwise cause suffering into something less significant.

These release theories have as their common base the idea that laughter results from a psychic release from tension, anxiety, frustration, and other harsh realities of life.

4. *The pleasure theory.*

Lois was carrying on an ordinary conversation with her three-year-old. Suddenly, in the middle of a sentence and apropos of nothing, Melissa began hopping all about, chortling with glee.

"Bug," she yelled. "Bug. Bug."

But there was no bug anywhere in sight.

For several weeks after that at all sorts of inappropriate moments, Melissa would begin to laugh uproariously as she bounced up and down like a rubber ball and yelled, "Bug. Bug."

No one ever figured out why. No one had been talking about bugs. Melissa did not seem to be competing for attention. She apparently received pleasure simply from shouting the word or from the image the word conveyed to her mind.

A laughter of greeting may also belong in this category. On occasion as I meet my dear friend Beth I laugh in recognition as we approach each other for a greeting. This involves no feeling of superiority or scorn, no incongruity, no relief of tension. Just joy in friendship.

What could be more central to humor than the idea of pleasure? One of the most significant characteristics humor possesses is its ability to lift our spirits and lighten our mood. Surely there is a laugh of simple merriment or joy.

Researchers Chapman and Foot (1976) have

suggested that the relationship of laughter to joy must not be overlooked. They believe that much of children's laughter, particularly during play, might be regarded as a pure expression of the joy of living.

Laughter can also signal rejoicing in God's goodness and can indicate gratitude to him.

Humor is closely linked with hope. As long as we keep our sense of humor, we can face our problems because we can look forward to the day when they are over—or we can at least put up with them.

Humor is also closely connected with the Christian virtues of joy, peace, and praise (Flynn 1960).

Author William Hamilton has said that our Christian defenses of humor have been a pathetic attempt to keep in step with a secular culture that has nothing else (*The Christian Century*, 8 July 1959). He believes that for the Christian, humor becomes joy.

But surely joy does not exclude humor. Humor is not displaced by joy. Rather it becomes one of the forms by which we express our joy.

The Bible gives examples of both mocking, derisive laughter, and the laughter of joy.

Examples of laughter are given in the Old Testament, many of them in the Psalms, where scoffing looms large. God is pictured as laughing, but with scorn at evildoers (Pss. 2:4, 37:13, and 59:8).

However, in Psalm 126:2, a picture of joyous laughter is presented—rejoicing in God's blessings.

The Old Testament endorses a merry heart, which would surely indicate some humor (Prov. 15:13, 15:15, 17:22). The Hebrew word used in these verses means "gleeful" or "joyful."

An interesting judgment is passed against the Israelites in the book of Deuteronomy. "Because you did not serve the Lord your God joyfully and gladly in the time of prosperity, therefore in hunger and thirst, in nakedness and dire poverty, you will serve the enemies the Lord sends against you" (Deut. 28:47, 48).

But enough, lest I wind up pulverizing our poor frog.

If you think about humor for a while, you will realize that humor includes surprise, feelings of superiority, release, and pleasure—and so much more!

We have now thought about our frog in several different ways. Perhaps we will be better able to appreciate him and wiser in understanding his purposes.

Of course, humor is not the answer to all problems. It is not, as one writer has called it, our ultimate hope. As our opening Scripture verse indicates, there is a time to laugh but also a time to weep.

As any would-be humorist quickly discovers, it is not easy to be funny all the time—or wise. What one person thinks is funny may be sacrilegious to another. A normally acceptable jest used at an improper moment when people are not in a playful mood may be taken the wrong way.

Joking and laughter can be used to cover up real feelings and even mask an insecure personality. People can joke to avoid facing an issue when in reality a deeper level of communication is needed. Then there is always the possibility of wounding another person, even when you don't mean to.

However, let's not brand God's gifts as wrong

simply because they can be misused or abused. We don't have to avoid humor simply because it can be potentially dangerous. We can ask for God's help to use it correctly.

Even so, some people still insist that humor is at best irrelevant and occasionally even harmful. Some think joking should be confined to the comic strips. Some writers even think the funny part should be stigmatized by three exclamation points so everyone will know that line is not to be taken seriously!!! However, humor is such a valuable asset that it deserves a place in the mainstream of life.

Now, let's explore the place humor can play in our families.

2

Filling The Family Purse With Laughter

"The boundary lines have fallen for me in plea-sant places; surely I have a delightful in-heritance" (Ps. 16:6).

Welcome to the world of Winston County, Alabama. It's July 1, 1861.

At a mass meeting of county citizens at Looney's Tavern in the county seat of Houston, the follow-ing resolution was drawn up and soon overwhelmingly approved:

> We think our neighbors in the South made a mistake when they attempted to secede. . . . We are not going to take up arms against them; on the other hand, we are not going to shoot at the flag of our fathers. . . . Therefore, we ask that the Confederacy on the one hand, and the Union on the other, leave us alone . . . that we may work out our destiny here in the hills and moun-tains of northwest Alabama (Winston County mimeographed history).

Then old "Uncle Dick" Payne, one of the few Confederate sympathizers present, made his satirical but historical remark, "Oh, oh, Winston secedes [from Alabama]. Hail, the free state of Winston!"

Some of the citizens of Winston County at that time were my maternal relatives or were later intermarried with my family. I feel I understand my family lineage and values better because I have heard this somewhat amusing historical story. I can appreciate my mother's family better because I know the story of "Uncle Dick" and other independent freethinkers who were trying to eke out an existence in the hardscrabble hills and piney woods of northwestern Alabama.

I also feel I belong to those people, though I am seven hundred miles and more than a century removed from the scene.

This is only one function, and not even the most important function, that humor can play in family living. Interesting and humorous anecdotes continue the family heritage, build a sense of family, and give that warm and secure feeling of belonging to someone somewhere. If you try to pass on your family history in other ways—preaching about "the good ol' days," for instance, or sermonizing on the glorious virtues of past family members—you may find out that the whole narrative is boring and even somewhat unbelievable, especially to teen-agers. Sometimes the best way to teach children your family story is by telling them about some of its humorous events and celebrations.

We all need to feel that we belong. Psychologist Abraham Maslow (1970) has put human needs into a scale from most to least important. At the very top of the list are life-and-death issues such as the need for food and water. Then come needs for basic physical safety and security. Next in importance is a sense of belonging and of being loved.

When our physiological and safety needs are largely met, we start thinking about giving and receiving love.

After we feel that we belong to someone, that someone cares about us, we can then give some attention to our self-esteem and self-actualization. We are then ready to achieve individual fulfillment through the creative use of our potential. But many people have to be concerned about their most basic needs, and thus never have time to think about their more refined needs, the ones that make us most fully human.

If we want our family members to reach those levels of self-actualization, we need to be sure the base is established. Their basic physical needs must be met. They need to feel they belong to a unique and special family unit.

Jay Schvaneveldt, a Utah State University sociologist (Lobsenz 8) who has studied the importance of family rituals in hundreds of families, points out that families with the strongest ties have the most celebrations and rituals. He stresses that customs are important not so much for what is actually said or done but rather for the sense of "we-ness" that grows out of the shared experience. The family ritual is a drama of how family members feel about one another.

Perhaps the most frequently repeated phrase used in connection with families is that sentence from the Russian writer, Tolstoi. "All happy families resemble one another; every unhappy family is unhappy in its own way."

Do you agree or disagree?

Like many oft-quoted generalities, what he says seems to contain a piece of truth but not the whole truth. The laughs and joys of families come in as many surprising ways as do their sorrows. In fact, one can hardly find anything odder than the unique and often wacky ways in which families find their happiness.

The prize-winning poet Phyllis McGinley in *The Province of the Heart* writes that happy families may, on the surface, seem similar because they genuinely like each other. But they have one completely personal treasure. She compares it to a purse, full of domestic humor they have accumulated against rainy days. This humor need not be necessarily witty and may be incomprehensible to outsiders.

Mrs. McGinley mentions that her own family purse is well supplied. "Do you remember the picnic when the horse ate our lunch? Do you remember how Daddy dressed up in a white coat and tied a towel around his head when he took our temperatures?" All of us remember humorous family incidents like these.

No doubt many of you have by now dipped into your own treasure chest of memories and pulled out the one about forgetful Uncle George or that matriarchal but well-loved grandmother.

Whatever the memory, notice your feeling when you pull that memory to the surface. Isn't it marvelous to belong to a family? An imperfect, irritating, zany, hilarious, wonderfully unique human clan? There's the sense of belonging – that secure feeling of family.

Humor also helps to shape a group of blood-related individuals into the unity we call "family." Psychological studies have shown that within a group, humor can strengthen the sense of unity and solidify the group (Goldstein and McGhee 116–118).

Heartily laughing together at the same thing forms an immediate bond between family members. When we find the same things funny, it not only helps our interpersonal relationships, but it is often one of the first steps in their formation. Laughter does bring people closer together.

DENNIS the MENACE

"YOU ALWAYS SAY SOME DAY WE'RE ALL GONNA LOOK BACK AND LAUGH ABOUT WHAT HAPPENED. CAN WE DO THAT *NOW* ?"

DENNIS THE MENACE ® *used by permission of Hank Ketcham and © by News America Syndicate.*

One of my family circles started forming three days before Christmas a few years ago at Mother's house. The relatives came pouring in. My husband, three sons, and I had arrived the day before. The next day I opened the door again and again as Uncle B. C. and wife arrived, then Uncle J. B., then a longtime family friend, some assorted cousins, and finally my older brother and wife with his married son and family.

The door opened and closed until there were twenty-one of us seated in a circle in the small living room on the mild December afternoon. Many of us were on the floor wedged up against the gaily decorated tree. We included four generations from my mother down to her great-grandson who was about sixteen months old.

On the table in Mother's kitchen was a veritable feast: banana nut bread, pecan pie, peach cobbler, iced tea, Pepsi, fudge, homemade peanut brittle, and various makings for sandwiches. Every few moments someone would leave the family circle for a short time to grab another snack and then return.

The baby was toddling and had learned to say his first word, "bite," indicating he was hungry. This child, however, had a special "bite." With a surprisingly deep voice, his delivery style was fluid and strongly southern. "Baht, baht," he intoned as he lurched toward his Grandpa.

Grandpa pinched off a bite of baloney sandwich and stuck it in the baby's mouth. He chewed part of it, slobbered part of it, and toddled over to his mother. "Baht." His mother expertly turned down her glass of Pepsi (without looking) and gave him a drink.

The toddler then started back around the circle. He tapped great Grandma on the knee. "Baht. Baht." In went a crumb of banana nut bread.

Still drooling, he whapped me across the knee. In went a small corner of a piece of fudge.

After each few bites, this child would toddle back to his parents for another drink. Then he would start around the circle again. This procedure continued for about forty minutes. During this entire process, no one paid close attention to the baby. We went right on filling the family purse with treasure: debating, relating yarns, and loudly discussing any subject that came up whether we knew much about it or not.

Eventually, I began to realize that we were turning this child into a toddling sugar cube. I took pity. "Hey," I yelled. "Do any of your realize how much we have been feeding this baby?"

We all laughed as the last crumb of fudge slowly dribbled its way down his chin. The baby was diapered and packed off into the kitchen to play with his favorite toys—a couple of plastic milk jugs with dried beans inside.

Each Christmastime since, during our feasting, we have recalled this story with much pleasure.

What does this little episode tell my children about their heritage from their mother's side of the family?

We are Southerners. Pecan pie, homemade peanut brittle, peach cobbler, iced tea in December, initials for names—all this should have been a clue.

A strong point of emphasis is the table of rich food. Most of our rejoicing is done around food—great quantities of tantalizing, high-calorie dishes. As far back as I can remember, even with the poorest of us, long tables overflowed with mouthwatering food.

For company, we would serve two or three different kinds of meat, homemade breads, three or four different vegetables, plenty of potatoes, and always a variety of desserts. Hospitality for us is connected with food. Far more than simply satisfying our hunger, this is sharing for us, the sign of a generous heart, the passing down of tradition.

Among our number are talkative people who love debate, tall tales, and laughter. We do not go to operas or concerts for our entertainment. We entertain each other.

Some persons may also have noticed that we do not go to operas or concerts for our entertainment. We entertain each other.

The fact is, all my children recognize these truths without having been lectured about their heritage or ancestry. Their family legacy is something like a patchwork quilt, pieced together with colorful fabric, many of the scraps made up of humorous stories. But threaded through all the piecework is a strong sense of identity and love, and they are covered over with the security of belonging.

One point needs to be made clear here. We should not give young people the notion that their task in life is to preserve ancient familial values unless those values are truly worth perpetuating. We need not continue the family weaknesses— better they be embalmed along with our ancestors. We can and should, however, let our young people know that in their generation they will need to rediscover the values proven worthwhile.

When you look for help in filling the family purse, here are some gold pieces from the experience of other families:

• Each month on Sunday evening a family that enjoys cooking has a "secret supper" night. Several days before the supper, the family members draw slips of paper to see which course they will be responsible for preparing. They then shop separately and meet that evening in the kitchen to cook their surprises. A daughter says that although it may not be their best balanced meal, it's the one they enjoy most each month (Lobsenz).

• In another family children interview different members and make up a family scrapbook, including some of the humorous family by-lines and stories. They include such items as unique family names, jobs, celebrations, and heirlooms.

• One mother I know wishes to pass down her family legacy of a strong interest in the arts. In addition to the traditional activities such as finger-painting and coloring, once a year she puts her two daughters into their bathing suits (usually in winter so it's even more of a novelty) and leads them to the bathtub where she has little bowls of shaving cream colored with different food colors.

The girls get sponges and happily splash away. They can paint anything they want as long as they stay in the bathtub and on the surrounding walls covered with tile. When they have finished, the girls, tile walls, bathtub and bowls are all washed down easily and quickly.

• In my own family, now with two sons away at college, I watch especially for funny stories, jokes, or cartoons that stress some point that ties in with a longstanding family joke, trait, or other aspect of our family history. I save these and mail them regularly to the boys to add to their family treasure chest. This reminds these men away from home that they are still a vital part of our family and will always belong to this family unit.

God chose our inheritance for us (Ps. 47:4). He has given us all a family—a unique and special heritage. The good news needs to be passed on to the next generation.

Now with our purses well supplied, we will take a look at the state of our health.

3

Take a Spoonful Of Laughs

"A merry heart is good medicine" (Prov. 17:22).

For some years the famed American playwright Moss Hart was bothered with insomnia. Finally, he decided to consult a psychoanalyst. Pianist Oscar Levant wondered whether the sessions had helped.

"Not really," Hart admitted, "but my attitude toward insomnia is certainly much better."

Our attitudes about many of our physical and emotional problems should be better today because science has made tremendous strides toward solving them. We have more information than ever before concerning the requirements of our bodies for vitamins and minerals. We also know more about our need for love, security, and self-esteem. Columns that give personal advice regularly appear in our magazines and daily newspapers. Consumer groups provide us with information concerning additives and preservatives. Television spots give us phone numbers to dial during times of emotional crisis.

In recent years, research has also touched on the subject of humor. Case studies are beginning to show the truth of the marvelous proverb recorded so long ago in Scripture—a merry heart does good like a medicine.

Scientists who have studied the effects of laughter have reported measurable positive effects on several different bodily organs (Cousins 1979). Laughter has been credited for being (1) an aid to recovery after disease, (2) a promoter of muscle relaxation in fighting pain; (3) a benefit to the respiratory and circulatory systems; (4) an aid to digestion; and (5) a help to good emotional and mental health by fighting such feelings as fear, depression, boredom, shyness, and stress.

A modern case study concerning recovery after disease involved the longtime editor of the *Saturday Review*, Norman Cousins (1979). His story shows the role humor can play in tackling even a serious illness like his—a collagen illness of the connective tissue.

His healing involved positive thoughts, massive doses of vitamin C—and old-fashioned, uproarious laughter. In coping with his illness, he watched old "Candid Camera" reruns, and a nurse read to him from humorous books. He found that ten minutes of genuine belly laughter anesthetized him and gave him at least two hours of pain-free sleep.

Blood sedimentation rate counts were taken just prior to and several hours subsequent to the bouts of laughter. Each drop in the readings was small but cumulative, so that over a period of days the drop was significant. Cousins soon went back to a normal and busy life writing and lecturing.

Cousins is cautious about creating false hope in other persons who have similar afflictions, but he does give laughter credit for at least part of his recovery.

In another instance a young male polio victim in London was taken to a musical comedy. He had been breathing with the help of an iron lung for a year. The theatrical trip was an experiment to see whether the hilarious antics on stage could help him laugh his way back to breathing normally (Cross and Cross).

The boy remained in his iron lung during the performance. He responded positively to the comic on the stage. Although he did not know it was happening, his nurse would turn off the iron lung each time he laughed. The laughter started his chest muscles working again, and for twenty minutes he breathed on his own. In a repeat experiment, laughter resulted in forty minutes of independent breathing.

Recent evidence indicates that laughter may directly attack pain associated with such inflammatory conditions as arthritis, gout, and those resulting from certain injuries (Peter and Dana).

Laughter stimulates the brain to produce catecholamine, an alertness hormone. This arousal hormone stimulates the release of endorphins. They in turn cause the perception of pain to decrease. So, in effect, laughter causes the body to produce its own painkiller.

Our entire cardiovascular system also benefits from hearty laughter because it increases the oxygen in the blood. Laughter gives a vigorous workout to the thorax, abdomen, chest, and lungs. When laughter subsides, the pulse rate drops below normal and the skeletal muscles become deeply relaxed (Robinson).

James J. Walsh was an enthusiastic defender of the role of laughter in health. He comments:

> There seems no doubt that hearty laughter stimulates practically all the large organs, and by making them do their work better through the increase of circulation that follows the vibratory massage which accompanies it, heightens resistive vitality against disease (preface).

Dr. Walsh particularly suggests that laughing provides badly needed exercising, or massaging, of the lungs, heart, liver, pancreas, and intestines. He states that a majority of people beyond middle age probably do not laugh enough for the good of their hearts.

For centuries people have recognized that light, pleasurable laughter is one of the best aids we have to proper digestion of our food. When we were children, how many times were we told not to argue or talk about unpleasant things at the table? We know almost instinctively that we enjoy our meal more and the food digests better when our conversation is enjoyable and the company congenial.

Experiments have proven that worries, tensions, angers, and fears check the natural flow of digestive juices into the stomach. In one classic case in 1929 Dr. Walter Alvarez of the Mayo Clinic reported the case of a young man whose food had not digested at all after six hours as a result of a political argument in his fraternal lodge.

Laughter also plays a vital part in our mental

health. A hearty sense of humor reduces boredom, helps prevent self-pity, allows us to discharge extra energy, and fights fear, anxiety, shyness, depression, and stress.

Businessman Robert Owens was extremely concerned about his declining business. An acquaintance, George Ortega, expressed concern. As Owens faced his own worry, he gained a better perspective.

After thinking over the matter, Owens replied, "You're right. I'm booked so solid on worries right now that if anything goes wrong today, it will be at least ten days before I can get around to worrying about it." With a hearty laugh and the realization that his anxiety was not helping matters any, he felt able to approach his problems more creatively.

Deborah Leiber, a registered nurse and instructor in the nursing school at Oregon Health Sciences University, believes it is important for her to help her students and patients laugh. So she created the NFL (Nurses for Laughter). Her organization encourages the use of humor that does not humiliate or poke fun at them in health care for patients. For instance, NFL has a professional cap day where all the nurses wear funny caps. Laughing helps relieve anxiety in the patients and lessens depression (McCarthy 1983).

When my youngest son was three, he had the grandiose idea that the whole world revolved around himself. He quite often expected his two older brothers to bow down and worship at his throne, but they quite often proved to be rebellious and disorderly subjects.

One day, a fiery volcano of an argument erupted in our family room in front of the television set. Being quite a distance down the hall and in the kitchen, I at first heard only the faint rumblings. As the heat increased, the top blew. Then the core of the blowup became clear. The little one wanted his own way. His brothers disagreed.

After thoughtfully considering the matter for at least two seconds, I did what weary, jaded mothers sometimes do—I took the easy way out and decided to let them settle the issue themselves. The hot molten lava of recriminations, accusations, and counter-accusations flowed all about the room.

However, the older two boys had size, age, and power all on their side. Eventually, the little guy was bound to lose. He stomped out of the family room, firmly planting one indignant foot down after the other, and marched toward the kitchen. With tears forming in his eyes, he pleaded with me to help him get his desire. For his own good, I refused.

When he finally saw that all hope was gone, he whirled his stubborn little back around and angrily whoomped out of the kitchen, this time waving an impudent small fist in the air. In sharp staccato, he briskly declared: "Well, all right then. Nobody around here likes me anyway. I'll just go give myself away."

We fight self-pity like a pox around our house, but it still occasionally strikes us down. Teenagers sometimes throw pity parties for the suffering member. "Everyone together now. Let's hear it for so-and-so. Boo, hoo, hoo, hoo, hoo." (This usually works best with me. I find it irresistibly funny when I see two huge, hairy-faced juveniles huddled together, loudly boohooing.)

At other times we drag out one of our funnies. That's what I did with my three-year-old in the story related above. "All right, then, no one around here cares anyway. Just go give yourself away." Then a hearty laugh drives the blues away.

But most of us realize these methods won't always work. Sometimes self-pity gathers strength until it turns into a relentless river that cannot be dammed. It simply has to have time to flow out to the sea.

On other occasions, however, when the sufferer cannot resist a laugh, we have stopped the whole pity process before too much flood damage is done.

PEANUTS by Charles Schulz, reprinted with permission from United Media.

There is, however, such a thing as unhealthy laughter. Uncontrollable laughter can even be a sign of hysteria and various forms of mental illness. When someone laughs at an inappropriate time or in inappropriate places, that is abnormal. It is a sign of mental illness and needs to be treated.

Some humor can be deeply hostile and insulting. In addition, humor that makes us less likely to do something constructive about an unjust or evil condition is sick humor. This book speaks of normal, merry, healthy laughter.

A person with a healthy sense of humor is capable of seeing himself and others objectively. He sees his or their foibles and laughs at them. Yet he remains in contact with reality and is emotionally involved with other people in caring ways. Such a person can go about life in a generally playful, joyful spirit but does not lose respect for himself and others and will not cheapen the precious and holy things of life.

Humor has spiritual benefits, too. It can keep you hoping. It can also be an element in praise. Healthy laughter can reemphasize a belief at the worst of times that God is ultimately good.

"May the God of hope fill you with all joy and peace as you trust in him, so that you may overflow with hope by the power of the Holy Spirit" (Rom. 15:13).

So far we have been talking about a genuine Christian ministry through humor. That reminds me of an incident connected with my ministry in humorous writing. One day while I was on a speaking tour, Brenda came up to me with the following story.

Her mother had an elderly friend who was in the hospital dying of cancer. The older woman was in almost constant pain. Brenda's mother decided to read a few pages to her friend on each afternoon visit. She had been reading my book, *I Need You Now, God, While the Grape Juice Is Running All Over the Floor* (1975). One chapter in particular had reminded her of her dying friend's background.

So she took my book to the hospital and read that chapter to the dying patient. At first the older woman chuckled, then began laughing out loud. After the reading, she noticed that for the full ten minutes of reading time, she had been unaware of her pain—her first pain-free minutes that day.

For several days after that incident, her friend continued to read to her from the book, and she learned to look forward to that time for relaxation and a short time free of pain.

A week later she grew worse, lapsed into a coma, and died. Here was an obviously critically-ill person who experienced relief from pain through humor.

I had a chance later to check out the effect of humor on pain in my own life. My husband, three sons, and I decided to spend one of our Christmases among the cacti in Arizona visiting my husband's parents who had retired there.

The night before Christmas Eve, I noticed a pain in my stomach. I didn't feel like eating, even with all the Christmas goodies around. I couldn't sleep through the night because the pain grew worse. By morning I knew something was wrong. At noon on Christmas Eve, I was being wheeled into the operating room for an appendectomy.

I felt depressed. Who wants to spend Christmas

day in the hospital? During a holiday season, everyone looks forward to fun with the family. We do not see my in-laws very often, so I had looked forward to this rare Christmas with them. Besides, I was two thousand miles from home. There I would have had friends to send flowers, visit, commiserate, pray, and joke with me. But I was not home, and even my immediate family would have to leave before I would be discharged from the hospital.

I resented missing Christmas. I wanted to be home. I was experiencing all the difficulties of a week-long hospital stay: being hooked to an IV machine, not being able to sleep, enduring the side effects of medication. How would I cope?

Most important, I had a spiritual faith that sustained me. I had experienced a deep abiding sense of God's presence and care. I decided to see if my sense of humor would help, even through pain and medication.

While my three boys were still in Arizona, they helped immensely. They joked regularly. They came up with the sickest (pardon the pun) kinds of puns. "Hope everything came out all right, Mom." "Don't laugh, Mom, you'll split your stitches." These were new puns to them, and they laughed heartily.

Then the guys became fascinated with my IV machine. Across the side were the letters IVAC, so they immediately dubbed the monster Ivac the Terrible. They laughed when they discovered I had to walk down the hall several times each day dragging this machine with me. "Mom's been out walking with Ivac the Terrible again."

They roared even louder when they heard I had

to sleep hooked up to the machine. The merriment reached its height, however, when they found that I was not unhooked, even to go to the bathroom. Ivac the Terrible was a constant friend.

I found that when I laughed with the boys, I felt better.

When I first felt like writing but the pain was still annoying, I decided to occupy my mind by making a list of titles for articles I would now be qualified to write. I worked assiduously for almost an hour before my energy gave out. I got many hearty laughs from my effort. That was the only hour that day when I was unaware of my discomfort. My list looked like this:

Ten Creative Ways to Wear a Hospital Gown
(I envisioned this one with cartoons)

How to Get the Attention of a Nurse:
Drop Off into a Genuinely Sound Sleep

I Don't Want to Get Younger, Just a Chance to Grow Older

Fit to be Tied: Life Story of an IV Machine

Digging in the Right Vein

An attendant joked with me the day before my departure. "I suppose you'll feel compelled to go home and write about all this."

"Indeed I will," I replied. "But rest assured. The book will *not* have an appendix."

Here are a few tips for injecting some humor into your family life:

• An acquaintance of mine with artistic talent makes her own posters to hang in the bathroom and bedrooms. They have had a carrot "pusher," a beast who adored broccoli, and a toothless troll who learned too late the dangers of not brushing his teeth.

• Norman Cousins reports that Albert Schweitzer always collected an amusing story or two during the day to share with the young doctors and nurses at Schweitzer Hospital in Africa during mealtimes. Life was not easy for them there, and they were reenergized by his pleasant, gentle humor around the table. One evening he shared the news that Edna, the hen, had six new baby chicks. "It was a great surprise to me," he related solemnly. "I didn't even know she was that way."

• A young mother I know always adds doses of laughter to the prescriptions for her sick children. She makes trips to the library looking for the funniest books and makes plenty of reading time during illnesses. Sometimes they even vote on the best story for the day and share it with Daddy when he comes home. The laughter prescription usually relaxes and refreshes Dad as much as it does the children.

Shared humor builds healthier people while it helps form closer bonds. It also encourages us to become more creative persons, as we'll see next.

4

Of Alpha Waves And Pickles

*"God saw all that he had made,
and it was very good"* (Gen. 1:31).

My seventeen-year-old son bounded up the stairs two at a time. "I've got it, Mom. I've got it. Let's write our own pickle jokebook. Here's the first entry. What is long, green, has two wheels and goes vroom, vroom, vroom? A motorpickle!"

He then erupted with laughter. That laughter was echoed by two younger brothers downstairs. We were off and vrooming.

Months before, my nine-year-old son had started bringing jokebooks home from school. He seemed to be stuck on food. First, he brought home a hotdog jokebook. Next came a small volume of hamburger jokes.

All three boys read the books. However, the two teen-agers groaned loudly all through and declared that they could certainly do better themselves. So now they had decided on a pickle jokebook.

I immediately latched onto this project as a

workable idea. For one thing it was six weeks
before Christmas and things were heading toward
a fever pitch at my house. With three boys, that
meant more teasing and fighting, less concentra-
tion on worthwhile projects, and more time
simply spewing off excess energy. The humor in
this idea of a jokebook had the possibility of
holding their interest for an extended period of
time.

Second, I had been casting around desperately
in my mind for some small token gift we could enclose in our Christmas cards. Now I asked myself,
what would be more appropriate than a small gift
of laughter for such a joyous season? Yes, I decided, we'll do the jokebook and run off copies to
enclose with our cards. Thus, our project was
born: *More Than You Ever Wanted To Know About
Pickles.*

I issued the challenge. In the next three weeks, I
wanted a hundred pickle jokes. Three brains
switched into gear and began a mighty uphill run.
As soon as they reached home in the afternoon
after school, they discussed pickle jokes. "Hey,
what do you get when a pickle drops out of
school? A dumber cucumber, ha, ha."

At the dining table in the evening, we rolled
smoothly along as we worked together on pickle
jokes. "What kind of bird is long, green, and
crazy? A cuke-koo." (Laughter and applause.)

Each night before I went to bed, I typed up the
output for the day. "What is a cucumber's favorite
musical instrument? A pickle-o."

Even when we were watching television, a
chance remark might trigger a train of thought
and a boy would suddenly spring straight up and

shout, "I've got it. I've got it. What did the mother hog call her baby when he fell into the vinegar vat? A naughty little picklet!"

When the mailing deadline came, we all agreed to settle for seventy-eight jokes. We were proud of our productivity. But frankly, my brains were getting pickled. Every time I saw a pickle, I turned green. I was fed up with pickles and encumbered with cucumbers.

Our small gift provided pleasure for others that Christmas. And for three weeks during the Christmas season, all the excess energy of the boys had been channeled into this creative project.

We need to encourage creativity in our children. Bold, original thinkers have done a lot for our world. Think of the influence of Beethoven, Michelangelo, Euclid, Thomas Edison, the Wright Brothers, Jonas Salk.

Where does such creativity come from? Sometimes it's the result of eccentric brilliance. Or perhaps it's the way our chromosomes happened to form. Sometimes it comes from sheer hard work. There are those who say it has to do with alpha waves in our brains. Perhaps in some people it is part of a great drive for power or fame. The Christian sees it as a special gift from God.

Whatever they accept as its source, people have generally recognized creativity as something worth having. It is part of being made in the image of God, our Creator.

Clyde Kilby, former chairman of the English Department at Wheaton (IL) College, in *Christianity and Aesthetics* (1961) considers the opening pages of Genesis to be the origin of the creative spirit in man. He links our imaginative powers and joy in creating to the Creator Artist who made us in his own image. Creativity can also be seen as a part of our God-given nature and our need to search for truth, beauty, and meaning.

What is creativity? Webster's *New World Dictionary* says it is "artistic and intellectual inventiveness." Creativity stimulates our imagination. When our children come up with some new idea that we have never thought of, we need to praise them and encourage them to do more. A friend of mine always tells the story of her six-year daughter asking at the time of moving from the only house she'd ever known, "Mommy, will the walls cry?" That's creative and funny in its own way.

THE FAR SIDE by Gary Larson, reprinted with permission from Universal Press Syndicate, © 1984.

In 1929, Sir Alexander Fleming, a British bacteriologist at the University of London, noticed that a bit of green mold had fallen from a plate in his laboratory. Most of us would have simply wiped away the mold. But because Sir Alexander had trained himself to look for the unusual, he noticed that the mold had destroyed the bacteria around it. If you or a loved one of yours has ever been saved from a serious illness by penicillin, you are probably grateful that Sir Alexander had learned to think creatively.

Creativity may be an unusual combination of quite familiar items. When my younger brother descended a ladder too rapidly using only the top rung, he fractured his arm in two places. The medical sling given him put too much weight on one part of his shoulder and constantly rubbed a sore spot there. Many people with broken arms have silently (or otherwise) endured such a circumstance. But my mother, who is not a high school graduate, quickly assessed the situation. Taking an old bedsheet and some pieces of wide elastic, she fashioned a new sling which distributed the weight more evenly. The doctor liked it so well he encouraged her to seek a patent. In any case, she had come up with a novel form of sling from old rags and elastic.

Jesus Christ presents the perfect model of creativity. His innovative thinking often confounded those around him who had been steeped in traditional values and taught to live by accepted patterns of thought.

Jesus was truly a creative thinker and teacher. He answered questions with other questions. He used illustrations and parables to stimulate creative thinking in his listeners.

He also used such forms of humor as irony, satire, and overstatement to stir up deeper thought (Trueblood 1964). He talked of a camel passing through the eye of a needle (Matt. 19:24) and of a man who strained gnats from his soup and then swallowed a camel (Matt. 23:24).

"True," someone may be saying. "But exactly what does creativity have to do with humor?"

The word *witticism* is derived from wit in its original sense of ingenuity or inventiveness. Even riddles and puns provide a useful side-door into the inner workshop of creative thinking. The very act of producing humor involves creativity.

Clinical psychologist Harvey Mindess says:

> The procedure of humor, in short, is the procedure of creativity . . . Most ordinary jokes and witticisms strike us as trivia. In themselves, many funny remarks may be nothing more than that, but as a body of activity, our indulgence in humor facilitates our creative possibilities, for it lubricates the unconventional, imaginative, problem-solving functions of our being.
>
> The play of wit puts pieces of thought together to create brand-new ideas. It pries us loose from encrusted ruts of thinking and invites us to skip along on novel pathways of the mind. It is in this respect that humor paves the way for originality on a wider scale. Our sense of humor has the power to unlock other creative potentials within us (p. 153f.).

Most theories of humor call attention to the element of surprise that results from creatively bringing together novel ideas—ideas that would not usually go together.

In your family you can train children to be more creative by encouraging their sense of humor. Creativity is, after all, a combination of flexibility, originality, and sensitivity to new ideas. And what better way to stimulate it than through laughter?

Arthur Koestler says the jester is genuine blood brother to the scientist and the artist. Comic comparison (humor) makes us laugh. Objective analogy (science) is to make us understand. And poetic imagery (art) is to help us marvel. Thus, creative activity can take one of three channels—humor, discovery, or art. In other words, Koestler believes humor is one of the three main branches of creativity.

This is not the place to be concerned with the difference between discovery and invention. Occasionally, someone with a quick wit will invent a new, humorous saying or story. More often we discover with delight some bit of humor someone else invented and modify it to suit our own purposes. But even this process involves an original combination. Though the parts of the joke may be familiar, the act of modifying it indicates creative effort on our part.

Many parents have noticed that creative thinking and a sense of humor often go hand in hand.

For example, Kevin had just returned home from a birthday party for his friend Robbie. Kathy, his doting mother, was anxious to find out if her lecture on manners beforehand had had any effect.

"Kevin, I certainly hope you didn't ask Mrs. Hudson for a second piece of cake."

"Oh, no, Mom," replied her resourceful offspring. "I remembered what you said. So I just asked her for her recipe, and she immediately gave me another large piece."

My own offspring have developed genuine talent in this regard. Once when I scolded a nine-year-old son for putting a filthy tee shirt back on after his bath, he quickly retorted, "But, Mom, the shirt was only dirty on the outside."

Getzels and Jackson of the University of Chicago tested 449 adolescents in a midwestern private secondary school for I.Q. and creativity (1962). From this testing, they chose two groups of about equal size—one with high I.Q.s but not very creative, the other highly creative but without high I.Q.s.

When they were asked to look at eight qualities and then rank themselves in the order in which they would like to be outstanding, the high I.Q. group put a sense of humor at the bottom, but the creative adolescents put it second from the top. The latter initiated humor more often. They also tended to have more imagination and playfulness, and, as might be expected therefore, a more highly-developed sense of humor.

These findings may raise questions in your mind. Did these young people have a good sense of humor because they were creative? Or did their good sense of humor help them develop their creativity? Perhaps both.

McGhee suggests that making jokes probably fosters the development of creative thinking, since a person must continually look for new ways to alter familiar ideas (1979).

How do we develop a capacity for humorous

thinking? Probably by enjoying life and being open to playfulness.

Here are some suggestions as to how you can use humor with your children and develop creativity in the process.

1. *The humorous catalogue.*

Spend your vacation at home, and your neighbors will recognize you for what you really are—sensible, imaginative, creative, home-loving—and flat broke.

In the family room one evening suggest inserting a funny item at the end of a list of serious items you can prepare in advance. Now try them on your family. I used this one recently in a humor workshop: "To have a child in your family means joy, delight, challenge, fun, and _____ ." I got answers such as "gray hair," "dirty diapers," and a "busted bank account." Maybe your family members can do better.

2. *Overstatement.*

Humorist Irvin S. Cobb used overstatement to good effect. He told about a horse he once rode from the Tudor period that had high dormer effects and a sloping mansard. He had been told the horse was sixteen hands high, but when he got on its back, he discovered it was sixteen miles high. What he had mistaken for the horse's blaze face seemed more like a snow-capped peak in the Andes.

This technique involves a vivid way of noticing and relating even the smallest details.

Practically all of us indulge in overstatement without being aware of it, but not usually humorously. "I've told you a dozen times," we say to a child when we have told him twice. "It's so hot today, I'm dying," a flourishing 170-pound teenager will say.

At times we may tread the thin line between fun and lying. I use this device only when I am fairly certain it will be interpreted in a spirit of playfulness and not literally.

I have used overstatement to describe what I think would be the ideal family car. This vehicle would come equipped with a twenty-gallon garbage bin, two strong straitjackets, extra backseat windows, a fully stocked snack bar, a working toilet, and a garden hose for cleanup. Some may call this exaggeration. However, any mother who has made a three-thousand-mile car trip with three pre-schoolers will know exactly what I mean.

To appreciate this kind of humor you can read funny stories with your children and point out places where overstatement is used.

You can also use incomplete sentences to develop their creativity with overstatement. For instance: the car was so old the insurance covered fire, theft, and Indian raids.

Now try your own.

He was so big . . . (he had to go down to the crossroad to turn around.)

She was so shy . . .

3. *Understatement.*

Item from a smalltown newspaper: A visitor to our fair city would have missed the noon train today, had he not stepped on a peach pit at the head of the depot stairs.

Perhaps the best example of all time, used very

simply in a title was Charles Lamb's essay, "On the Inconveniences from Being Hanged."

Now spark some imaginative thinking around the dinner table with understatement.

Few things so quickly modify neighborly love as . . . (a BB pellet through their car window.)

4. *Puncturing pomposities.*

An Indian from a reservation visited Chicago. While wandering around town he was stopped by a native Chicagoan who snobbishly asked, "What do you think of our big city?"

"Oh, fine," replied the Indian. "And what do you think of our country?"

Your children will likely bring home examples of this type of humor. You can also discuss the prejudice that may sometimes be involved in some of these stories.

5. *The sudden twist.*

A man who was wanted by the police had been photographed in six different positions and the pictures sent out to the state police. A few days later, headquarters received a note from a small town chief: "I duly received pictures of six criminals wanted. Five of them I have already captured, and I am hot on the trail of the sixth."

The method of the sudden twist involves a break in logic. The unexpected punch line is perhaps the most widely-used form of humor.

A woman appeared in divorce court. The judge reviewed the facts of the case. "You say you want a divorce just because your husband is careless in his appearance?" he asked.

"Yes," answered the long-suffering wife. "He hasn't shown up for five years."

This type of humor will be prevalent in the jokes family members bring home. You can discuss the creative thought involved in coming up with an ending that "double-crosses" our thinking. Or try to come up with other surprise endings.

6. *Sudden identification.*

A fellow staggered into the medical clinic with an arrow through his chest. He collapsed on the desk of the doctor's receptionist. She looked up coolly from her appointment book and said, "How about a week from Wednesday?"

Anyone who has ever tried to get an appointment with a busy specialist will laugh, though perhaps ruefully.

If you have ever been thoroughly lost, you will also laugh at this story:

"But they told me you were the best guide in the state of Minnesota," growled the tourist as they doggedly tramped through the deep woods.

"I am," replied his guide. "But I think we're somewhere up in Canada by now."

You can invite family members to share this element of identification by giving them a chance to post cartoons or jokes with which they identify. Significant discussion may grow out of these, and you can get to know each other better.

7. *Absurdity.*

Two little morons found a flashlight and were playing with it. Finally one of them found how to switch on the beam. He shined it toward the ceiling. "Betcha can't climb that all the way up," he said. "Nothing doing," replied his companion. "You'd turn it off about the time I got halfway up."

This category includes fantasy and any ludicrous escape from reality. Most children enjoy the typically American tall tales about Paul Bunyan or Texas and Alaska jokes.

During those long summer days when your children have too much time on their hands, some of them will enjoy writing their own tall tales. Give them a hand.

8. *Mutilated quotations and mangled cliches.*
A bird in the hand . . . (may get messy)
Children should be seen . . . (not hurt)
These axioms are fun for kids to think up. Throw out a list of old proverbs and see what they can do.
A penny saved is . . .
A rolling stone gathers . . .

9. *Puns, riddles, and other wordplay.*
How do you catch a rabbit? Sit in the garden and act like a carrot.

What else could one possibly say about riddles? When children are between seven and ten, they can riddle you faster than bullets. Before tearing your hair out, remember. Good creative interaction is involved. Have them make up their own riddles for a family newspaper or letters.

Number play is fun for keeping children occupied during long vacation trips. 1 1 1 1 8 1. What does the eight say? (I think I need to diet.) Make your own rows of numbers say something.

Or play the name-occupation game. What's a good name for a plumber? (Mr. Waterman.) Minister? (Doobie Good.) A surgeon? A cowboy?

While traveling, Laura, a friend of mine, has her children draw an imaginary animal (or critter from outer space). Then she then encourages them to create a funny story about the creature.

A judicious mix of creative and humorous thinking may not only lead us to pickles but also help us out of them.

*"I think her mom likes
me. She didn't take her eyes off
me the whole party."*

5

When The Gears Of Life Grind On

*"He will yet fill your mouth with laughter
and your lips with shouts of joy"* (Job 8:21).

In our family room two of my sons were loudly
arguing over which television program to watch.
Their voices grew more strident.

"Go get Dan."

"Why?"

"Because we need him to make the decision and
get the program turned on, while we finish our
argument."

With that perceptive statement, they looked at
each other, burst out laughing, and eventually
compromised agreeably. Humor had reduced a
mountain to a molehill and finally to a speck of
dust.

Life is full of specks of dust disguised as mountains. Nearly every day some rugged peak shows
up. As the old country song so aptly describes it,
"Life gets tedious, don't it?" Television programs
conflict, washers break down, the car won't start,
the bank or the post office closes two minutes
before we get there.

As the gears of life grind relentlessly on, we often need a solvent for the grit of irritation. Some days, coping almost takes more than we've got. What then?

Humor can be one of the best solvents because it helps remove conflicts that are traumatic in the short run but minor over the long haul.

A group of contemporary humor theorists led by D. Byrne discovered that people learn the habit of using humor as a successful coping mechanism. Since it is a pleasant experience, those who have had success using humor to cope will obviously tend to try it repeatedly.

On those tedious days, a hearty and well-rounded sense of humor is a priceless asset. Not only can it keep you from taking yourself too seriously, but it can also make it possible for you to handle those circumstances that otherwise might get you down.

The saints of old apparently discovered this truth. Morris Bishop in *Saint Francis of Assisi* (1974) tells us that St. Francis often celebrated joy. He justified his gaiety as a defense against the devil's tricks and felt that a gloomy soul was an easy prey for Satan.

Martin Luther, the great Reformer, was sometimes troubled by deep depression. For it he often prescribed dining with good company, joking, and singing. Luther believed the devil could not endure fun and gaiety.

If you lack a well-developed capacity for humor, you probably test out short on self-confidence and the ability to cope with stress. Appreciation of humor has been found to be a stable personality trait associated with maturity (O'Connell).

Harry Overstreet has commented on the role of humor in distinguishing specks of dust from molehills: "An incongruity is something out of proportion. . . . To see things in proportion and to be playfully aware of the incongruity is the wisdom of humor."

Dr. Overstreet suggests that people often exaggerate their own importance, say one thing while they do another, and in effect, make giant peaks out of mere protrusions.

Most of us note these inconsistencies and get irritated about them. But the humorist can, with a proper perspective, transform the irritating situation into laughter.

When Anatole France received the coveted cross of the Legion of Honor, he was still a poor man, having earned little from the sale of his books. As his friends looked at the famous sash, they became irritated.

"Why couldn't they give you some kind of cash prize?" one friend protested bitterly. "This thing serves no useful purpose at all."

"Oh, I wouldn't say that," replied France with a better perspective. "When I wear the sash, it will cover that permanent stain on my old jacket. That's helpful."

Humor can help us learn to deal with daily life. A lighthearted viewpoint on many of the annoyances that come to us daily can even help to develop the fruit of the Spirit (Gal. 5:22, 23) in our character—particularly patience, humility, and self-control.

In an article in *Reader's Digest* (May 1973) William Ellis, examining the advantages of humor, believes that humor is a most effective means of handling stressful situations. He suggests it can be used to patch up differences, apologize, say "no," criticize, gain cooperation, dissolve a hostile confrontation, and keep a small misunderstanding from escalating into a big deal.

Sounds useful around the house, doesn't it?

Leonard G. Epstein, a behavioral scientist at the Center for Human Development in San Francisco states that research has shown shared laughter to be an effective tension reducer in families (Isaac).

Laughter does not always enable us to change reality, but it can help us endure it. Humor may not remove our selfish egos and self-pretensions, but it can help us see how silly they are and get us to thinking about their absurdity.

As a coping mechanism, laughter does help relieve our tension. When people yield to a fit of laughter, they become physically limp. Many of us can probably remember a time when we laughed until we felt physically weak. For good reason.

The relaxation effect of laughter has been studied scientifically. When a listener first anticipates something funny and tries to think ahead to the outcome, there is a short-term increase in stress. This can be measured by peripheral skin temperatures and increased pulse and blood pressure.

However, twenty seconds or so after the laughter subsides, this effect begins to reverse. Tension continues to decrease for some time. The effects have been measured and have been known to last up to forty-five minutes. The greater the intensity of the laughing spell, the bigger the decrease in tension and the more long-lasting the effect. It is difficult to become anxious when the muscles are in a state of deep relaxation (Peter and Dana 60).

Laughter can also be an effective antidote for coping with the stress caused by an inferiority complex. Each of us is unique. And nearly always at some point in our lives, that very uniqueness will be a source of discomfort, pressure, or discrimination.

CATHY by Cathy Guisewite, reprinted with permission from Universal Press Syndicate, © 1983.

In studies sponsored by the Air Force, a researcher has observed that humor is one of several effective techniques that a creative person often can use to remain in a group and still resist group pressure toward conformity (Harper 1980). This person is accepted without conforming because he is funny.

By learning to relax and accept unchangeable weaknesses, we can gain a measure of respect. This then leaves more emotional energy for discovering and developing strengths, thereby adding to self-confidence.

A sense of humor encourages us to accept not only our own individuality but also the imperfections of others. We learn to accept the fact that these traits help define their personalities.

American writer John Erskine once said that humor is "the art of adapting oneself to another temperament." He suggested that once you have acknowledged the right of all your fellows to survive, even when they disagree with you, you must then learn how to adjust to their peculiarities without surrendering your own uniqueness.

Our humor can affirm our acceptance and appreciation of the world and its variety in human personalities. Perhaps the teacher who wrote the following note on what was otherwise an extremely poor report for a second-grade boy expressed the idea best: "He does contribute nicely to our group singing with his helpful listening."

Often when we joke about our klutziness, our cowardice, or our large nose, we are making an attempt to accept ourselves and our individuality. Our laughter will then sometimes bring a moment of objectivity when we see that others are also entitled to their assertiveness, their huge mouth, their timidity, or their naiveté.

Humor, then, is a factor that helps us get close to other people. Empathy is the state of understanding that results from one person understanding how another might feel in a certain situation. Empathy promotes healthy human relationships, and good relationships reduce the stresspoints in life.

A word of caution is appropriate here. Humor is not a panacea for all ills. We are talking in this chapter about molehills that seem like mountains. We are not talking about the Rockies. We have to learn to accept minor irritations. We have to be willing to respect and accept the other person's foibles. We need the ability to keep a proper perspective. But if bonafide mountains appear, family members will not appreciate our attempts to laugh them off by joking about them. Deep, sustained communication is essential in that case, and counseling may even be needed.

Some real-life research may prove helpful here. In a three-day period of time, I tried to observe the irritating situations in our family that the use of a bit of humor helped to solve or reduce. Perhaps these examples will suggest practical applications for your family.

• On Sunday morning in my rush to finish breakfast and get everyone ready for church, I didn't get the bed made. My husband could not resist calling this to my attention, though he knows I make a real effort and succeed most of the time in keeping it made.

I insist that he is compulsive in this matter. One

wrinkle in a bedsheet disturbs his equilibrium. The quilt has to be tucked in under the bed exactly one and three-quarters of an inch.

As for myself, I like a crumpled, comfortably wrinkled bed. It fits me better somehow. But I have largely given in to his insistence that a bed cannot be slept in with good health unless it has been immaculately straightened out during the day.

"Look at this bed," he said. "My. My. We're really on top of things today."

"Concerning beds," I retorted, "on top of it is definitely the best place to be." We looked at each other, laughed, called this round a tie, remembered our resolutions to bear with each other, and went on to other matters.

• I went out the back door to go to the drugstore. My car was blocked in the driveway. Again.

With teenage sons we have had as many as seven vehicles at one time. Two are in fairly good health. The rest are all near-terminal cases. I drive the car with the healthy pulse. But somehow, one (or two or three) of the sickies gets pulled in behind me. Our driveway is so narrow, I cannot go either way around the other cars. I had no hope this day but to try to move the automobile blocking my way.

I finally located a key and crawled in cautiously (so the spring sticking up through the upholstery didn't jab me). I checked the back door to be sure it was still tied shut with the rope. Then I turned my attention to the dashboard. Lo and behold, no ignition. Just a gaping hole. I looked around. The ignition was hanging loose on a wire down by the floorboard.

How badly did I need to go to the drugstore? Was it worth electrocution?

I carefully inserted the key and prayed. I turned the key slowly as I squeezed my eyes shut. If the whole thing blew, including me, I didn't want to see any of the pieces.

There was life in the old Studebaker yet. She growled, coughed a time or two, then began to chug-a-lug. I backed this catastrophe out on the street.

I then parked that car, went back to the driveway, started my car, pulled out on the street, parked it, got in the other car, pulled it back in the driveway (the street is being worked on), returned the extra key to the kitchen, walked all the way back out to the street, got into my car, and took off.

The drugstore is only five minutes away. But this day I spent fifteen minutes just getting started. Frustration had been rising. Suddenly as I thought over the whole matter, I roared. Ridiculous is ridiculous and deserves a laugh. And anyhow, one day the junkers (along with the teenagers) will all be gone, I'll have the driveway to myself, and I'll be looking for some place to go. I might as well enjoy the fun.

Laughter had helped me get things in proper perspective, and that saved my day.

• A spirited argument arose among the three boys around the table as to who was the dumbest. The banana pudding had started the brouhaha. "Ugggh," said the little guy, "banana pudding would be fine if it just didn't have bananas in it."

"What's wrong with you, anyway?" asked a bigger brother. "Don't you know every little kid likes bananas?"

"I'm not a little kid, and I don't like bananas."

"Yes, you do. You always used to like them. Then one day you just got it in your head suddenly to *not* like them. That's dumb."

"If you like them, you're the one who's dumb."

"They're good for you. Eat em! It's all in your head."

"Yeah, I guess that's my problem. I've gone bananas."

All three boys laughed aloud. End of argument. Mother was not forced to intervene. Laughter had ended another stressful situation.

Lloyd Ogilvie in his study of Philippians mentions attending the Vinnette Carroll musical, "Don't Bother Me, I Can't Cope," at the Huntington Hartford theater in Hollywood. He remembers the audience galvanized together as they were walloped again and again with their weak excuses for not becoming involved with people and with the crises of society. He suggests that the motto of a Christian should be just the opposite. "Go ahead. Bother me. I can cope."

Those who are followers of Jesus need to remember they can cope. "I can do everything through Christ who gives me strength" (Phil. 4:13). We have this source of unlimited power available to us through Christ. In addition, we have God's gift of laughter to help us through our days, even those days when the gears of life grind noisily.

Go ahead. Bother me. See if I can cope.

6

Learning With Laughter

"Pleasant words promote instruction"
(Prov. 16:21).

A young man in the hills of Tennessee made a wager with friends to spend Halloween night in an old haunted house out in the country. He decided ten dollars would be worth the discomfort. As dust settled over the hills, he and his friends slowly walked down the winding country lane to the stark, gloomy old house.

By the time they arrived, the moon was casting eerie shadows through the tree branches in the yard. He left his companions, and with already reluctant feet and regretful heart he cautiously inched through the front door.

A loose shutter banged around on its squeaky hinges. Spider webs covered large portions of the ceiling. Moonlight from the huge yellow harvest moon outside glowed through the window. In one corner was a grimy old sofa with broken springs. The young man gingerly poked around until he found a place to sit. He then settled down uneasily on the couch to see if he could last out the night.

He surveyed the spider webs. He crossed his legs. He uncrossed his legs. He decided to count to one thousand. He ineffectively tried to ignore the hundred and one spooky sounds squeaking, swishing, grating, rattling, shuffling, and clanking around him. The seconds flew by like days.

Just as exhaustion was beginning to take over and the young man dozed on the couch, a huge black cat ambled out from behind a door and seated itself beside him.

"Good evening," said the cat cordially. "Sure is a nice night we're having. Glad to have company here in this lonely old house for a change."

"Forget the company, cat," stated the young man with emphasis. "If you don't know how to run, you'd better learn because you and me is about to have us one whopper of a race." He jumped up and took off down the lane with all the speed he could muster. The glossy black cat loped effortlessly along at his heels.

The lad increased his speed until finally he could feel the hot breath on his neck no longer. He collapsed on a tree stump in an exhausted frenzy, gulping for air. Just as he lifted his eyes, he saw the cat cresting the nearest hill, gliding gracefully along.

The cat sat down beside him on the gnarled black stump. "Sure was a good race we had there, wasn't it?" said the cat pleasantly.

The young man recoiled like a spring and with a new spurt of adrenalin began to sail down the dark dirt road once more. "Listen, cat," he yelled back. "We ain't had us even half the race we're gonna have."

This was the end of my favorite Halloween story. Mother never went any further with the narrative. I had fun trying to imagine an ending.

Years later, I was in college and at the end of my tether. My money had run out. I was physically exhausted from working long hours. A college degree no longer seemed worth the effort.

"Shall I quit?" I asked myself. For several days, a battle raged within between hope and despair. Then with determination welling up from somewhere deep inside, I very clearly heard these words with the ears of my mind: "Listen, cat, we ain't had us even half the race we're gonna have."

I gritted my teeth, prayed for strength, jumped up from the stump, and raced on toward graduation. A funny story about an old Tennessee backwoodsman and a black cat had unexpectedly come to my aid.

Yet years later I stood by the side of a desk as a young son of mine wrestled with some difficult homework. He was ready to give up. Too hard. An unfair assignment anyways, he insisted. Dumb old teacher. Why does she make us work so hard?

We took a short break. I told him about the Tennessee hillbilly and the black cat. We both laughed.

"We're not quitters in our family," I ended. "We always give the cat the best race we can." He gritted his teeth, plopped down at the desk, resumed his effort, and eventually puzzled out the homework. An important personality trait was being taught with a spirit of fun.

Although humor should always be done with a spirit of fun, it is not always merely for fun. Humor can be coupled with instruction, persuasion, discipline, and other facets of the educational process.

Whether the classroom be at school, in the home, at church, in the woods, at the zoo, or in any other place in God's universe, those of us who have worked with children in any way know that a sense of humor can improve our teaching. Creativity, motivation, enjoyment, a positive teacher-student relationship, and a disciplined but loving atmosphere with reduced tensions create the ideal learning situation (Robinson 1977, 93). In the different chapters of this book we see that a sense of humor makes the ideal situation even more ideal.

You cannot begin too early to help your child develop a sense of humor. At five and six months of age, my babies pealed with laughter as I recited parts of alphabet books with funny sounds. They especially loved the explosive consonant sounds such as *b* and *p.* We roared together at Dr. Seuss's "painting pink pajamas" and "Peter Pepper's puppy." We delighted in some of Edward Lear's nonsense rhymes. I found later that I had given my children an excellent foundation in phonics well before they were a year old. They all became early, excellent, avid readers.

Educator Carl Rogers states that a sense of humor is one of the essential qualities of a teacher. Being genuine is an essential characteristic of a good teacher. Rogers sees a sense of humor as one aspect of being genuinely human. This is not to say that every teacher (or parent) should stand in front of her scholars and tell jokes, especially if she tells them poorly. But it does indicate that she needs to have a playful, imaginative, and flexible attitude toward learning.

ANDY CAPP   **by Reggie Smythe**

ANDY CAPP by Reggie Smythe © 1984 Daily Mirror News-papers Ltd. Distributed by News America Syndicate. Used with per-mission.

Communications theorist Marshall McLuahn makes a point that I have often thought about. He questioned why learning has long been associated only with serious people. He suggests that our age presents a unique opportunity for learning by means of humor. A perceptive joke can be more meaningful than platitudes lying between the two covers of a book.

We might also consider the words of Ralph

Waldo Emerson: "We must learn by laughter as well as by tears."

An interpretation in the form of a joke often disarms a person and bypasses his resistance. It also has the added advantage that the hearer may be left to figure out the message for himself. This increases his learning and memory retention.

Experimental studies on humor to inform or persuade on a short-term basis suggest that humor does not increase our learning. But it sure does increase our interest and keep our attention.

On the other hand, a humorous lecture had a definite effect on test scores in San Diego State University psychology classes (*Family Weekly*, 19 February 1978). The students heard a nonhumorous lecture or one of three others containing humor. On a quiz immediately after the lectures there was no difference in student scores. But a retest six weeks later showed higher scores for those who had heard the humorous lectures.

Learning in the home usually takes place over a longer period of time. More teaching is done over a long period of time, and humor would seem a logical tool to reinforce points, relax the learner, and altogether make the learning experience more enjoyable for both parent and child.

Abigail Jungreis states that people like to listen to someone with a sense of humor. Information that's presented in a funny way has a better chance of being remembered than a list of facts (*Scholastic Update*, 14 October 1983).

In an interview with *U.S. News and World Report* (18 October 1982) Laurence J. Peter, educator turned humorist and satirical writer, argues that relevant humor is valuable in teaching. If you can illustrate a point you are making with a humorous anecdote, people are more likely to retain it.

Certainly in my experience as parent, teacher, writer, and public speaker, I agree that humor gains attention and aids retention.

Philosopher John Morreall of Northwestern University believes that the main features of humor, especially its connection with imagination and creativity, are valuable in all education. Teachers often do not try to cultivate playfulness or imagination in their students. They have been taught that life is a serious business, consisting basically of a series of lessons to be remembered and problems to be solved. Life is fundamentally doing one's job. Thus children who start school when they are five years old and full of playfulness, imagination, and curiosity have often lost these qualities within a couple of years (1983, 98)

Morreall suggests that instructors integrate humor into the learning experience. Students will then no longer be mere receivers of prepackaged information but curious, playful, creative human beings who experiment with ideas, ask outlandish questions, and even make wisecracks. The rewards of this kind of teaching can be rich.

Those of us who are parents, as the prime educators of our children, have an even better opportunity because of the intimate relationship we have with our children, plus the fact that we have a smaller number of children to work with.

Goethe once said that there is no more significant index of a person's character than the things he finds laughable. I would like to suggest, also, that the things we laugh at can perhaps help build our character. We can use humor not only to teach facts, but also to inculcate spiritual values and ethical standards.

One of the most valuable teaching incidents in our family concerned a purchase made by our youngest son on vacation. He was about five at the time and had two dollars, which to him was untold riches.

We had never before been able to get across the state line on vacation until this child would spend all his vacation money. This time we managed to talk him into waiting until we got to the first Indian trading post. Then he would wait no longer.

He decided to buy a rubber-type hunting knife encased in a cheap plastic sheath. We tried to bargain with him. "You're wasting your money. How about an Indian headdress? You could wear it for Halloween. Or how about a nice addition to the rock collection?" But alas, no. He had to have the hunting knife.

We were traveling in a pickup truck with a camper shell on back. Summertime had arrived, so the small slatted windows in the camper were open and the three boys were riding in the back.

Shortly after reboarding the truck, our son got too close to the window in the back and out went the plastic sheath. The boys could not get our attention in the cab soon enough to stop and retrieve the holder.

Very shortly after this catastrophe, someone sat down on the knife and broke the handle off the blade. Within the hour, my five-year-old's purchase had become a useless plastic handle and a flimsy rubber knifeblade, good for nothing.

I expected tears, but none flowed. That night

when we stopped in a restaurant, the other two boys recalled the incident. As they talked, the story got funnier and funnier. I looked to see if the younger one was insulted. Instead, he was laughing as loudly as all the rest.

He still remembers that vacation as the time when he wasted his money, and a small reminder of the "bladeless knife without any handle" still helps him be more cautious with his spending. Even the older two boys occasionally bring the story out, dust it off, retell it, laugh heartily, and use it to remind themselves to be wise spenders.

The book of Proverbs in the Old Testament is an excellent teaching tool with good humorous possibilities. Its pages contain many amusing sayings that will stick in the minds of children.

Our favorite is Proverbs 26:13-15, which concerns laziness. The lazy man says, "I can't go out. There might be a fierce lion roaming the streets." This lazy man even buries his hand in the dish because he is too lazy to bring it back to his mouth.

Proverbs 28:1, contains the laughable picture of the guilty man who flees even when no one is chasing him. Here is a good springboard for a discussion of true moral guilt, the effect it has on our lives, and how to be forgiven.

The nurturing of values that decides society's stand on order and morality and religious faith is going on every day in our families. These values, for good or ill, are being nourished in our modern media, in our classrooms, from the clamorous marketplaces, in our publications, and out of the bowels of advertising agencies. The family that abandons its own role of instruction, of nurturing the standards and the faith of its young, will find that function taken over by other forces in society. But will you like the end product?

As the most important teachers of our children, we parents should be willing to use every teaching tool at our disposal. Sometimes learning with laughter will be the most effective way of getting our message across to our children.

Here are some suggestions that I have found to work for others.

• An artist friend makes humorous posters. Such posters are an effective teaching tool since the human mind tends to retain far more of what it sees than what it hears. For instance, a personable walrus teaches good toothbrushing habits by proclaiming "Get those molars shining white." If you're not an artist, sometimes good posters can be purchased.

• An acquaintance was tired of nagging her children about piling the dining table full with books, toys, and other assorted paraphernalia as they came home from school. When she went to set the table each evening, she needed five minutes to clean off debris. Nagging never seemed to help.

Then one day, she conceived the glorious idea of setting the table (including best china and candles) in the morning just after she cleared the breakfast dishes. Voila! No more room to pile anything. The children learned tidier habits by being reminded in this way to take their belongings to their rooms.

• A schoolteacher decided to try out a new way to keep her students together on field trips. She had not been able to do so on earlier outings and had experienced considerable anxiety when some child would stray from the group temporarily. On the next field trip, she simply announced as they pulled out of the schoolyard, "If you get lost today, the bus driver will eat your lunch." The children stayed close together and occasionally reminded each other, "Hey, you'd better keep up or the bus driver will get your lunch."

7

Facing The Lie Detector

". . . and the truth will set you free"
(John 8:32b).

A couple of years ago I found myself in a theo-
logical seminar for "deep-thinkers" (how I got in
this situation is beyond explaining). One young
seminary student came up with a question that
the four panel members (all experts in their field of
study) couldn't even understand, much less answer. The question was tedious, terribly hypo-
thetical, and couched in the most ostentatious
terms – it was clearly meant to impress. I laughed
aloud at this pedantic young egghead.

Then, suddenly a memory of a similar situation
in a college classroom when I was a freshman sur-
faced. The theology professor was getting old and
perhaps just a bit senile. I threw him with my ob-
scure question and felt very clever. Years later,
further down the road to maturity, I realized my
question had been unnecessary. I had begun to
learn by then how much I didn't know.

In remembering the incident I laughed again,

but more ruefully this time. The humor of my own experience had confronted me with a contradictory aspect of my personality.

Such an experience may hit us with the pleasure of instantaneous understanding as we chuckle. On the other hand, it may momentarily ruffle our egos, and we pensively laugh as we say "ouch." But behold, another glimpse of truth has been fitted into our life experience. An insight has come and we are now in a position to do something about it, even if it means changing some aspect of our own behavior or personality.

Theologian Karl Barth maintains that humor is the opposite of all self-praise. Barth says that humor and humility go hand in hand to draw sinful human beings away from pretentiousness and pride. It is the overly-proud person who cannot laugh at himself for he must maintain his dignity at all costs.

Humor can be an enlightening experience involving self-discovery (Fry). It can be used redemptively. Humor becomes redemptive when it leads us to self-discovery, and that self-discovery then sends us searching for God or for more of God's truth.

Browne Barr, a Congregational minister has suggested that by means of the collapse of human pretensions God may be reminding us of something important for our deliverance. God is God and we are persons. God is infinite and we are finite. Even bishops who step on banana peels are subject to the law of gravity (*Christian Century*, July 1976).

When our own limitations are exposed, we may become angry or despair. Through faith we can learn that anger and despair are not the only responses to human weakness. God may send laughter to lead us away from an undue preoccupation with ourselves.

A humorous perspective may even include a prophetic warning against idolatry—against the greatest blasphemy, the claim to possess or to be as God (Hyers 223). Humorous remarks remind us of our mortality, finiteness, and foolishness. In this sense, humor is not all play. It may contain an important element of prophetic seriousness. Sin, for example, is surely harmful and therefore to be treated with sobriety. However, sin is also foolish and may, on occasion, be treated comically to show us how ridiculous it is.

Humor is an effective lie detector (Lorenz). Humor can be honest, usually without arousing anger. Through the spectacles of humor we sometimes see the foolishness of our sin, the folly of our own self-pity, and the pomposity of our self-righteousness. Humor helps make the world a more honest place. We can use it to help ourselves and our family members face reality.

Pianist Ignace Paderewski humanly enjoyed praise. However, when adulation was overdone, he reacted unfavorably. Once following a concert, a gushy woman rushed up to him and began to pour out a number of saccharine comments. She finally ended with, "You must have an extraordinary amount of patience to learn to play the way you do."

"Oh no, Ma'am, not at all," replied the pianist, "not at all. I have no more patience than anyone else. I just decided to use mine."

Humor at its redemptive best is this kind of

heightened truth – truth made so vivid our minds simply cannot escape it.

HAGAR THE HORRIBLE

Reprinted with special permission of King Features Syndicate, Inc.

In all honesty, we must admit here that joking and laughter can also be used to evade truth. But we do not refuse to use other of God's gifts because they can be misused or abused. We simply learn to use them correctly.

In spiritual matters, more than in any other realm perhaps, we become acutely conscious of sharp inconsistencies in human behavior. Humor can help us come to the point where we accept reality and face ourselves as we truly are—needy people in the presence of a holy God.

Psychologists at the University of Massachusetts found that persons who made the best scores on sense-of-humor tests had the best insight into their own personalities (Harper). They had a greater ability to look at themselves objectively. The person who cannot laugh at her or his own imperfections may be afraid to look deep down inside and face the truth.

Perhaps we can profitably explore at this point the way humor is used in the Bible to reveal truth. We do need to understand that the Bible is not a definitive textbook on humor, of course.

Thirty-eight times the Bible makes reference to the words *laugh, laughed, laughing, laughter* (Talmage). However, some twenty-five or so of those references refer to scornful or empty laughter. The remainder of the verses may refer to joyful, meaningful laughter. No fewer than six of them come from the story about the birth of Isaac. The word *humor* does not even appear in the Bible, so we will find no full analysis or detailed theology of humor there. Scripture does, however, supply some good examples and help us to understand the uses of humor.

In 1 Kings 18, especially verse 27, we see that the great prophet Elijah had a sense of humor. He skillfully teased the priests of Baal with the impotence of their god. The miracles that follow clearly speak for the truth of his side.

The prophets of Baal cried out to their god to consume the altar with fire. But no matter how loudly they screamed their god did not hear.

Elijah could have then said simply, "Okay, boys, now it's my turn." But no, we are amused by Elijah's taunts, which reveal the truth of the matter. "Pray louder," he yells. "Maybe your god is daydreaming or perhaps he's off on a trip. Could be he's sleeping. Better see if you can't wake him up!" The truth is that their god was permanently asleep. He could not consume the alter in fire, but Elijah's God could.

People have always been fascinated by the idea of talking animals, and in this century we have had a spate of movies about Francis, a talking mule, and also a television series about Mr. Ed, a talking horse. But the book of Numbers in the Old Testament beat them to the idea. In chapter 22, we are presented with Balaam, a well-known and supposedly wise prophet. When the angel of the Lord blocked the road of the prophet, the wise man did not recognize the angel, but his faithful donkey did. The donkey stood still as if literally rooted to the ground until the angel opened up the way.

A second time the angel appeared. This time the donkey, beaten by its master, crushed Balaam's foot against a stone wall. When the angel appeared for the third time, the donkey again saw what the wise prophet could not see. This time she simply lies down on the road and flatly refuses to move. Hardly anything is funnier than a stubborn mule or cow that places its bulk down somewhere and refuses to move (unless, of course, you are the one responsible for moving the animal).

Eventually the angel of the Lord gave the poor dumb creature the power to speak, and only then does the "wise" man see what the animal saw long before. Here is an interesting truth revealed in a humorous manner. Sometimes it is easier for the Lord to reveal himself to a dumb animal than to a person who knows too much (Grotjahn).

One of the times laughter is directly mentioned is in the context of an amusing story in the first part of Genesis 18.

An angel of the Lord announced that Sarah would bear her first child to her husband, Abraham. Only one big problem. Sarah had qualified for Medicare twenty-five years before.

Sarah first laughed a laugh of unbelief. The Lord kept his promise. The child was born a year later and Sarah named him Isaac, meaning "laughter." But now the laughter of unbelief had become the laughter of joy.

For Sarah, it must have been the laughter of sheer delight and thanksgiving. We can assume that the neighbors laughed with her, not only out of good-natured surprise but also with genuine pleasure and hearty good wishes. We, too, laugh with her, though the truth presented here (that nothing is too hard for the Lord) is a profound and serious truth.

In the Gospels and the teachings of Jesus we see truth often revealed through the use of humor— largely ironical humor. Our laughter here may turn into a rueful smile.

Christ was dead serious when he battled for the lives and minds of people. Thus we can believe he would use the best tools and the sharpest weapons at his disposal. He frequently used parables, homely little stories about common objects with which ordinary people could identify. These parables are often subtly humorous (Trueblood).

We also see him again and again using humor in
his dialogue with people for the purpose of reveal-
ing truth. Christ encountered bigotry almost from
the beginning of his ministry, and he used the
sharp weapon of ridicule against it. We can hardly
help but laugh at some of his assessments of the
hypocritical Pharisees, although if we allow the
truth to seep all the way into our own consciousness, we may soon be saying "ouch" again.

Let's look at a few short examples.

Matthew 7 contains an important truth: we
should be extremely cautious about judging
others.

"Do not judge, or you too will be judged. For in
the same way you judge others, you will be
judged, and with the measure you use, it will be
measured to you.

"Why do you look at the speck of sawdust in
your brother's eye and pay no attention to the
plank in your own eye? How can you say to your
brother, 'Let me take the speck out of your eye,'
when all the time there is a plank in your own
eye?" (Matt. 7:1–4).

Unfortunately this story has lost its vividness to
most of us. We have heard it too often and ap-
proached it in a somber and "religious" mood.
Such an approach causes us to miss the humor.

But any child can tell you. Trying to take a speck
out of your friend's eye when you have a large
plank in your own eye is truly funny.

In Matthew 23, Jesus uses the humorous techniques of exaggeration and irony to teach a very
vivid truth: we often become so concerned with
externals and minor points of law, we forget the
more important things.

"Woe to you, teachers of the law and Pharisees, you hypocrites! You give a tenth of your spices—mint, dill and cumin. But you have neglected the more important matters of the law—justice, mercy, and faithfulness. You should have practiced the latter, without neglecting the former. You blind guides! You strain out a gnat and swallow a camel.

"Woe to you, teachers of the law and Pharisees, you hypocrites! You clean the outside of the cup and dish, but inside they are full of greed and self-indulgence."

A mental image of the setting will cause an outbreak of laughter. Here we have this fussy man with elaborate and meticulous care polishing and shining the outside of his cup. What's so funny? The inside is filthy. What do we ordinarily do when we wash a cup? Why, we wash the inside because that is where most of the messy part is. But this man continues right on washing the outside and leaving the inside dirty.

Here's our legalistic man again. This time he is straining his soup because he has found a gnat in it. He gets out his strainer, an extra bowl, and perhaps a spoon in case the gnat slips through the strainer. He goes into careful detail as he makes doubly sure the gnat is strained out.

Now here's our incredibly fussy man once more —the same guy who just strained his soup. But this time without paying any attention at all, he is swallowing a camel.

A camel is a sure sign of God's sense of humor in creation. The ridiculous nose and mouth, down it goes—then the humps. Just for fun, let's make it a two-hump camel. As it goes down, we see the man with two Adam's apples instead of one. There goes the wooly thatched carpet on the humps—I can almost feel it tickling as it goes down his throat, but still our fussy man does not notice. He is so satisfied that he strained out the gnat.

Finally, those bony knees bob down the throat like softballs, and there go those absurd padded feet. Our man of the hour keeps drinking his soup, still looking for gnats. He has never once noticed the camel.

I can't help but laugh. Then a disturbing truth comes creeping close to the edge of consciousness. Can I face the truth? Could Jesus have told the same story on me? Have I ever strained out the gnat and then swallowed a camel—without even burping? Would I do such a stupid thing as washing the outside of a cup without cleaning the inside? Would I?

The truth has worked its way into my consciousness. I am now responsible for facing it. I realize I may have washed the outside of the cup a time or two. But how did the camel get down without my tasting it? I now have the opportunity to grow through this new insight. The humor of Christ's teaching has served to bring me closer to God.

When the Bible is read with an observant mind, plenty of things can be found to smile about. However, in many of these cases even as a smile appears, that "ouch" factor will take over. We are faced with some truth pertaining to our character or spiritual condition. Then we become responsible for responding to that truth.

Try these suggestions.

• Pick out a Gospel (Matthew, Mark, or Luke) to read around the dinner table for a few weeks. Have family members watch especially for truths revealed through humor.

• Have family members collect cartoons to share where some basic truth of life is taught in a humorous fashion. Then invite them to make some cartoons of their own to be posted on the refrigerator or bulletin board.

• Helen Lightstone, educational services manager for the *Chicago Tribune*, suggests that you have a child imagine he's a Martian landing on the earth, and he has only the comic page to learn about such things as values, jobs, relationships, food, and family life. What kinds of values would he discover about us earthlings? (Knutson, 2 March 1984)

How would these values fit in with God's truth? Discuss any changes that should be made in your family lifestyle.

8

Of Recorders and Warm Laps

"Better a meal of vegetables where there is love
than a fattened calf with hatred" (Prov. 15:17).

During World War II a chaplain from one company observed one of "his boys" quivering from head to toe. To comfort him, he said, "Don't worry, son. Every bullet that comes over here has a name on it. If it's got your name on it, it'll get you, no matter what. If it doesn't have your name on it, then there is no need for you to fear."

"Yes," replied the young soldier. "I know that—but what worries me are those bullets marked 'To Whom It May Concern.' "

Soldiers often express their fear during war with favorite humorous stories. Laughter is a potent form of communication and can be used to express an astonishing variety of human emotions. Anxiety, fear, embarrassment, concern, hope, and joy are all emotions frequently expressed through humor. Laughter in itself is a kind of language.

However, researchers have found that certain

cues indicate when humorous communication will usually work best (Robinson, 164). Some of these cues would be a previous joking relationship, a tone of receptivity indicated by smiling or twinkling eyes, or a general feeling of warmth, openness, and trust. Humor seems to communicate best when all persons concerned are in a playful spirit.

When humor is initiated in a nonhumorous setting, a joke-frame should be established by either verbal or non-verbal cues such as a smile, twinkling eyes, a shift in posture, a small chuckle, facial changes, or a lighter tone of voice.

In her doctoral dissertation Margaret Mullaly researched the nature and structure of humorous communication between four pairs of adult sisters.

The development of humorous interaction in their lives contributed to their relationship in a purposeful way. Through humor, their sense of belongingness deepened. The unique quality of each pair's humor also revealed the intimate nature of their relationship.

In short, humor is a marvelous way of relating with warmth and belongingness. It can be used in many ways to express love.

Laughter of the genial, hearty type conveys a goodly portion of kindness, acceptance, and a desire to reach out and communicate. A mirthful spirit can be a source of joy and encouragement to others. And family affection seems to grow when freedom is allowed to laugh with each other.

Laughter can say "I love you" when other forms of communication are not acceptable. I have been learning this lesson since my older boys became teenagers. I have always been a rather ooey-gooey, mishy-mushy, huggey-kissey kind of mother. When my boys were smaller, they were very longsuffering with me in this regard. I simply helped myself to a generous portion of affection whenever I pleased, and they tolerated yukky Mom.

Then both boys grew bigger than I am. Now I have these two gangly, raw-boned, maddening, marvelous, wacky, witty, frustrating, fascinating, half-man-half-child persons in my family.

Now how do I say to them, "I love you. You are really a precious person to me. I am so proud to share my family tree with you"? Believe me, it isn't always easy. But I am learning more often to resort to humorous ways of giving out the message — which they readily accept in that form.

One Sunday in connection with a sermon on love, our pastor happened to mention a workshop he had attended. In this workshop research had been presented showing that children need at least eight minutes of physical touch each day, and adults about four minutes.

I seized at this opportunity to jest with my big boys. "Wow," I said at the dinner table. "I had better ask Pastor how many minutes of touch teenage boys need each day."

The next time we saw our pastor, I jokingly asked him. He aided and abetted the situation by insisting he was sure teenage boys would need at least eight minutes of touch per day.

I badgered, and they demurred. Finally one son found a satisfactory solution. He acknowledged

Mother could not possibly stand by and watch her boys grow emotionally starved. So one handshake would stand for each minute.

We now shake hands eight times a day. If you see mother and son some day shaking hands and grinning, laugh with us. Laugh and remember this. We are communicating our love in a way acceptable to my teen-ager. We are saying to each other, "I like to touch you. I really do care."

Humorous communication often promotes love and harmony by eliminating nagging.

The ugliest thing about nagging is that it does often indicate an attitude of superiority, a bit of undue pride. "Why can't you do that right?" (meaning "I know how it should be done. You goofed.")

This problem can often be avoided if we carefully watch our own motivation and find a humorous way to make the suggestion. Humor can be a way to provide constructive and loving criticism without destroying our child's self-image. We can often use humor to point out mistakes and express values while we still preserve the self-esteem of the other person.

Laughter can help indicate a loving relationship rather than a judgmental attitude. "Oh, well," laughter may say, "possibly there is a better way to do the job, but you'll learn. You are not an awful person. Just imperfect—like me."

The comic spirit can bring us together as fellow sinners. Comedy jars us with the evidence that we are really no better than other people. Therefore we have no sound basis for destructive nagging.

A traveling salesman once walked into a restaurant and said to the waitress, "Bring me some burnt toast, a watery scrambled egg, and some weak, cold coffee."

The waitress said with some doubt, "Yeah, sure. What else would you like?"

"Just sit across from me," the man pleaded, "and nag me. I'm terribly homesick."

Perhaps for a few lucky men and women, their family members or friends feel unloved without a little nagging. For most of us, however, our family will enjoy us more without it. So when a point absolutely has to be made, we can learn to say it once, say it softly, and say it with humor.

Studies have shown that children nearly always laugh and smile more when they are in the company of other people (McGhee 205). They are sensitive to the presence of a companion and to the spirit of those present.

This might suggest to us that our children will be happier as they enjoy communicating with the rest of the family than if they are left alone (perhaps in front of the television) most of the time. Our children deeply sense our attitudes and perspectives on life.

In 1981, *Redbook* reported the results of a study by two professors at the University of Nebraska in Lincoln. Nick Stinnett and John DeFrain designed this research to look at 350 happy families to establish what characteristics they had in common. This happy-family profile turned up six key points. In considering these, we might be able to see what part humorous communication and interaction can play (Milofsky):

(1) Happy families spend time together. Professor Stinnett observes that by spending time together pleasantly, families build up a reserve of

good feelings. They may find their fun in simple ways, working in the yard together, taking a walk, playing table games. He stresses that when trouble comes, it nearly always has to be shared with the family. Thus it is important that the reserve of shared pleasures already be there to balance the troubled times. If the joys are not there, people will come in time to associate family life with problems rather than enjoyable things.

(2) Happy families have good communication patterns. The family members spend a lot of time talking to each other. They feel free to bring conflicts out in the open. Laughter can help balance the times of conflict.

(3) Happy families show appreciation for one another. Natural patterns of showing appreciation and accepting it are part of the supportive behavior of these stable families.

(4) Happy families are committed to the family group. When these families found they were no longer enjoying each other, they crossed other things off their priority list and made the family top priority for a time. Learning to enjoy each other does take time and commitment.

(5) Happy families tend to be religious. Most of the families in this study had a strong religious orientation. Stinnett points out that this does not necessarily mean a nonreligious family will be unhappy.

However, he does refer to other research conducted over the past fifty years that shows a strong correlation between religion and happiness in all phases of life. It seems clear that religion can be a major source of strength for families. We have mentioned in previous chapters the correlation between humor and such Christian virtues as hope, joy, and peace.

(6) Happy families deal with crises positively. Two points were prominent. These families had the ability to focus on something positive in every situation, no matter how bad.

Secondly, they joined together to face crises headon.

One question considered in the Family Strengths Study is whether these six traits can be learned by other families. Stinnett feels that unhappy families can improve their relationships by observing and emulating the communication patterns of successful families. People who have never associated family life with fun and joy can be shown how to enjoy each other.

Inside a marriage, humorous communication can be used in many ways to say "I love you."

One woman used a rather unique method of communicating. Her husband was a construction worker who brown-bagged it for lunch. For years, this man and his coworkers would sit around the site somewhere and relax at noon while they ate their lunches. Coworkers noticed a small bite always missing from this man's sandwich as he unwrapped his lunch.

For a long while, no one dared ask him about that missing bite from the corner of his sandwich. But curiosity ran rampant.

Eventually a new worker came on the scene who didn't mind asking personal questions. He came right out with it. "Why do you always have a corner of your sandwich missing?"

The worker laughed. He had grown so used to the custom, he had never thought to explain. Now he did so.

When she fixed his lunch, his wife simply used this way to say to him each day at noon, "I'm thinking about you." The small missing bite was her communication to him. "I care about what is happening to you today while we are apart. I love you."

The smallest things count. Cookies with funny faces say "I love you." Funny stickers for a favorite bicycle speak of love. Humorous cards at unexpected times bring encouragement and love as well as the gift of laughter.

A five-year-old pony-tailed moppet loved *Winnie the Pooh.* She especially liked to sit in Daddy's lap while he read to her. As Daddy's assumed voice for Piglet and Eeyore sounded forth, her young voice would peal with laughter.

Then Daddy got tired of *Winnie the Pooh.* A dozen times, two dozen times he read about Winnie, and his daughter still wanted more.

One day Daddy was seized by the most marvelous idea. He would record Pooh Bear with all the assumed voices on a cassette. He would then teach his small daughter how to push the bright red button and turn the pages. Presto! Instant Pooh.

At first, the child was entranced with the pretty red button. One slight push and Daddy's voice instantly issued forth.

Then the novelty of the whole situation began to wear off.

On the fifth day came a small knock at the door of Daddy's home office. "Daddy, read Pooh."

"What's the matter, honey? Daddy's awfully busy. Did you forget how to push the button?"

"No, Daddy. I can still push the button on the recorder, but I can't sit in its lap."

No question about it. Stories are just funnier when another person is close by.

How many delightful ways can you say "I love you" to someone this week? Here are some ideas that have worked for others.

• An acquaintance of mine plays a variation of Charlie Brown's *Happiness is a Warm Puppy* with her family to help communicate their love for each other. At special times together she has different members finish the sentence "Love is . . ." Many of these responses are humorous. Love is . . . (giving something besides sweaters for Christmas). Love is . . . (your brother letting you have the biggest cookie).

• I sometimes clip comic strips to communicate certain messages. This method can be effective if not overdone. Rather than constant nagging about messy rooms, I recently clipped the picture of Mrs. Flagston (of the "Hi and Lois" comic strip) with her T-shirt bearing the motto "Please clean up your room" and posted it in a conspicuous place on my son's bulletin board. With a smile and lessening resistance, he started cleaning his room.

• A woman I met at a workshop has developed a specialty of leaving amusing notes for her family when she is away. Creativity in placing these notes goes far beyond the usual shaving mirror or pillow. One note was discovered underneath the cover of a frozen casserole she had left to be cooked for supper. Another found its way to the top of the Ajax can. This was not only a note of reassurance but also served the purpose of finding out whether the sink got scrubbed as assigned.

• Another workshop participant found a unique way to communicate to her family that it is okay to act silly occasionally.

Once a year, on the grayest, most depressing day of winter, she suddenly announces that this is the day of the "silly party." If possible, they call other families in their apartment building or friends nearby and invite them to the party that evening. Then they quickly plan the silliest food, costumes, and games they can think up for the occasion.

One year, Daddy rigged up a towel with a big superhero "S" on it, found some gray pajamas, made some mouse ears, and attended the party as Silly Mouse.

Will those children remember all the expensive toys and gifts they receive through the years?

Probably not.

What will they remember?

The time Daddy was Silly Mouse.

They ask to see the pictures every few months.

• Another acquaintance told me how her Mom used humor to communicate to them how special they were. Her family lived on an isolated farm, and the three children had no other kids to play with and very few social events to attend. So in addition to each child's regular birthday celebration, they each got to have a nonbirthday. Each sibling chose the day of the year he or she wanted a non-birthday party.

Nonbirthday gifts could only be homemade items or objects found around the farm such as pretty rocks or leaves. Nonbirthday cakes were just as delicious as birthday cakes but were decorated in unusual ways and without candles.

The nonbirthday child, of course, chose the menu for the day. I didn't ask if they also sang a nonbirthday song, but I have had a lot of fun since then trying to write one.

Through the sharing times in humor workshops I have found that there is hardly any message that cannot be communicated through humor. Zany people with wacky ideas are running around in the most unexpected places, and only the slightest encouragement will often bring on mild forms of insanity. If you have a burning message to get across and all other forms of communication have failed, try something funny.

9

The Laughter of Faith

"A cheerful look brings joy to the heart. . . .
(Prov. 15:30a)

"From there to here, from here to there, funny things are everywhere," wrote Dr. Seuss. A profound truth stated simply. Parents who fail to explore the funny things everywhere with their children are missing a genuine source of joy and closeness in their family life.

For years I explored funny things with little boys. Mud was fun, so we had special mud days when all boys could play in the mud in as many ways as they wanted for as long as they wanted.

We had a celebration complete with special cake, when one boy found the first hair on his chest.

We acted out many of our stories. I sprawled on the floor smack in the middle of the small males, pounding the floor with despair and loudly weeping crocodile tears when we read about a sad king.

Amazingly, through all those years, the little boys thought I was the normal mother and all the other mothers on the block were the abnormal ones. But I did wonder occasionally about my own sanity. So I was comforted when I came upon Bernice Schneyer's study of mothering styles.

Dr. Schneyer found that a readiness to relax and enjoy the ridiculous helped compensate for other deficiencies in mothers. Humor served as an adaptive mechanism and eased the stress associated with parenting. The mothers who had the most and least interest in humor also demonstrated respectively the most and least effective parenting.

Bruce Ebert conducted an informal study in which he asked practicing family therapists to describe their idea of a healthy family. The answers listed a sense of humor right along with such factors as sharing and understanding feelings, caring, cooperation, acceptance of individual differences, and having an overall philosophy of life.

The beneficial effects of shared humor between parent and child are widely acknowledged among psychologists (Isaacs). Considerable evidence has been collected to show that a cheerful outlook is an invitation to interaction from others. Ready humor can indicate goodwill and break down walls, therefore contributing to honesty and openness in relationships.

If a sense of humor is such a valuable possession, how then do we get it? In a study of a hundred pairs of twins, researchers from the London Institute of Psychiatry found that the family environment appears to be the most important factor in developing a sense of humor (Wilson, Rust, and Kasriel).

We cannot at this time seriously suggest a specific gene for passing along humor, so we come back to the familiar combination of heredity and environment. We can also add to these factors a deeply-rooted joy that overflows from a firm faith in God and his ultimate goodness.

If parents enjoy playing with words and punch lines, if they laugh a lot, if they are always looking for the positive and delightful scenes in life, if they have a good sense of perspective, if they feel good enough about the world in general to approach it at times with a playful attitude, their children are far more likely to do so.

Nevertheless, we can hardly deny that some people seem to be born with more of a quality of exuberance and a spirit of good-natured playfulness than others.

The Canadian humorist Stephen Leacock touched on this matter:

> Few people know anything about humor, or analyze or think about it. It is left clean out of the program of self-improvement. A man will work hard on such things as his game of golf. It is pathetic to see a stout man trying hard to improve his mashie shot, a thing which God forbade to him at birth. But still he tries. Yet would he ever seek to improve his sense of humor, ever practice his funny story, or ever read a book on how to tell one? For all other literary and artistic acquirements there are classes and courses, schools and colleges. . . . But no one teaches funny boys humor.
>
> Granted that an innate aptitude is required for real excellence, it is equally true that it may be indefinitely improved. . . . Teaching humor would not mean teaching people to make fun of

things, but teaching people to understand things. Humor, at its highest, is a part of the interpretation of life (pp. 3, 4).

Psychologist Allan Fromme states that the best way to learn the habit of laughter is like the best way of learning a foreign language: not by taking courses, but by living with people who practice it. Dr. Fromme also believes when we learn to laugh at some difficulty, we can actually feel different about it. By changing our behavior, our feelings follow. Thus laughter helps us maintain a sense of proper perspective and a sense of balance.

The best way to develop a sense of humor to its full capacity is to relax and slow down a bit, try to keep things in proper perspective (keeping a close watch out for specks of dust), be less tense mentally and emotionally, and look for signs of God's goodness.

Laughter is surely among our blessings. Through our many anxieties that never develop, through the fears that do come to pass, in the myriad strains and pressures of our modern-day society, through our daily disappointments, irritations, and frustrations; time out for a short period of hearty laughter or even mild amusement may help throw off the poisons of depression, pessimism, and ingratitude that so often infect our minds and bodies. Laughter supplies diversion, refreshment, and good fellowship. It may even supply a colorful and pleasing touch to the character-picture that each of us is engaged in painting with his or her life.

Some sociologists are now suggesting community centers with a "humor" and "play" environment where people could go and enjoy themselves in a wholesome way.

A group of students at King Alfred's College in Winchester, England focused upon creating a humor environment.

GEECH

GEECH by Jerry Bittle; reprinted with permission from Universal Press Syndicate, © 1984.

These students got permission and cleaned out a basement area in the boiler room under the college. Various settings were available where people could enjoy themselves—a spaceship, a submarine, a theater, and a central area where cos-

tumes were available to dress up with, strips of
jokes and cartoons could be viewed, and people
could add to a continuing story on a large roll of
paper. A sizeable collection of props were available such as false moustaches, glasses, noses, and
goatees.

The basis of the idea was to see if people would
feel better after passing through a specially designed room—a place to relax and enjoy themselves and where each person would be encouraged to exercise her or his own unique sense of humor.

Seventy percent of the testing sample of 103
people said they definitely came out feeling better
(Chapman and Foot 1977).

Judith Horstman tells us that we now have a humor museum in the works in the United States.
When this museum opens in Le Claire, Iowa, not
all the ears of grain in that state will be turned into
livestock feed and cereal. The $15 million humor
museum will contain both corny and classic main-
stays of American humor including Fibber
McGee's closet, Will Rogers monologues, and
continuously running films from the Marx Brothers and the Three Stooges (*USA Today*, 6 February
1984).

Some people who accept the idea of a humor
museum in Iowa, however, will have more trouble accepting the idea of humor as an integral part
of a Christian outlook on life, including its signifi-
cance in family relationships.

Humor that profanes the sacred must be differ-
entiated from humor grounded in faith. Laughter
without faith may lead to irreverence, cynicism,
and despair.

Faith without laughter, however, may lead to dogmatism, depression, and even the worst kinds of intolerance.

One only need remember the barbarous history of inquisitions, heresy trials, witch hunts, religious persecutions, and holy wars through the annals of Christian history to realize the shocking possibilities of total devotion without any saving sense of humor, humility, or perspective.

Holy laughter is born out of belief in a meaningful universe, but the bitter laugh arises out of a meaningless void. The holy laugh is at the finite bonds that now imprison us but not forever; the bitter laugh is at the ultimate because everything is meaningless.

An ancient custom in Greek Orthodox circles set aside the day after Easter as a day of merriment, a day in which joking and jesting were considered appropriate within the sanctuary because of the big joke God pulled on Satan in the resurrection (Hyers, 156).

Indeed God does have the last laugh. In Eden and again on Golgotha, the demons must have thought they had made the fate of the human race one of never-ending seriousness. But God has turned it into celebration.

C. S. Lewis has pointed out that pleasure is God's invention, not Satan's. Satan cannot produce long-lasting pleasure. All he can do is to encourage humans to use in the wrong ways, or at the wrong time, or in degrees which God has forbidden, the pleasures that God has given them. God created pleasure. God means us to enjoy life's good gifts.

Nevertheless, we need to be vigilant in teaching

our children to avoid the misuse of laughter and humor. Immoral and injurious humor should surely be avoided.

Joseph Bayly suggests that we avoid (1) laughter that hurts another person, (2) laughter that short-circuits times of intimate fellowship, and (3) laughter that masks our real feelings and personalities.

It should also be noted that laughter can be used to "laugh things off" where change or restitution would be more in order. It can also become an easy path of escape from accountability or serious intellectual labor and commitment.

How then do we teach our families to approach the areas of humor and laughter in a way that pleases God?

(1) By recognizing God as the creator of the laughter mechanism. God has made us with the possibility of enjoying humor.

(2) By remembering to thank God specifically for the gifts of humor and laughter.

(3) By always using humor in a way that glorifies God and shows our enjoyment of him and his creation. God has given us an environment with touches of the comical (consider a camel, a penguin, a cactus, or a porcupine). We can then safely assume that it is okay to laugh and enjoy God's creation.

(4) By pointing out that God's book contains examples of humor. A theology of humor could possibly be built around the concept of joy so prevalent in the New Testament. *Joy, joyful,* and *joyous* are mentioned at least sixty-seven times in the New Testament. Joy is listed as part of the fruit of the Holy Spirit. An interesting aspect of joy in the

New Testament is that sorrow and trials can enlarge our capacity for joy (2 Cor. 8:2 and James 1:2). Therefore, we may find reason to laugh even amid life's problems.

(5) By refusing to use, or allow our children to use, humor in abusive or destructive ways.

(6) By remembering that God grants humor a place inside redeemed human nature because of the nature of his grace and as an expression of joy, praise, hope, and deep-seated peace.

Laughter can even confirm our forgiveness. We are accepted in spite of our unacceptableness because the chasm between the imperfect and the perfect has been bridged by Jesus Christ (Vos 69). We feel free to laugh at our finiteness and imperfections when we have surrendered to the Perfect and Infinite. In this way, our laughter can be grounded in the amazing grace and mercy of God.

Those who belong to Christ need to remember that Christianity is ultimately a religion of great joy. Christians laugh and sing not because they are blind to suffering and sorrow but because they know that these are not eternal realities. Though Christians will certainly be at times sad, disturbed, concerned, or confused, they can never be worried about the ultimate outcome of things. They do not deny tears but rather affirm the happy truth that outlasts all tears. God's truth will be triumphant, so believers can afford to let their joy and laughter burst through.

When laughter and humor are understood in this fashion and based in God's love and grace, we cannot afford to miss teaching our children the laughter of faith.

Here are some places to gather humorous and

delightful news to share with your family at the end of the day:

• Simply tune in on others. Learn to listen for the funny. Develop a special talent for listening to children.

A visiting minister asked five-year-old Jennie, "Where is Jesus, Jennie?"

"How in the world would I know?" replied Jennie smartly. "But if you really do need to find him, you probably should start by looking in Bethlehem."

• Look at billboards and signs. A man in Los Angeles once looked up at an apartment window. A sign there read: "Drums for sale." In an adjoining apartment window, another sign proclaimed: "Thank God."

• Pick up humorous items from television and radio. Some news reports include amusing human-interest type anecdotes toward the end. A local station in Louisiana once reported that out of fifty guests at an anniversary party, more than thirty had been married to the same man for at least twenty years. It would be interesting to hear how the poor man coped.

• Look for boners and goofs in newspaper headlines, church bulletins, school papers, and letters.

"Doctor Compiles List of Poisons Children May Drink at Home," one newspaper declared.

A church bulletin proclaimed: "All the youth choirs of Our Redeemer have been disbanded for the summer with the thanks of the entire church."

• Jot down your own humorous experiences of the day before you forget them.

My nine-year-old son once arrived home on his lunch hour from school and collapsed in a perspiring heap on the nearest chair. With a dramatic flourish he entreated, "Mom, get me a pen and paper, quick! I've got to write Dear Abby."

When we got to the bottom of his problem, he was basically bored with school. But his remark certainly relieved some of my own housework tedium that day and helped keep me from needing Abby's counsel.

• Collect cartoon quips, especially those relevant to your own family interests and jokes.

Some small choir boys were gathered around their pastor, begging him to help them start a baseball team: "And, pastor, could we use the bats the sexton said you have in your belfry?"

• Books and magazines will often contain humorous items you can share. Never overlook biographies. Real people are often funnier than fiction.

Abraham Lincon was once criticized during a debate for being two-faced. "I'll leave that to the audience to judge," he replied. "If I had two faces, do you honestly think I would be wearing this one?"

• Don't forget to report some aspect of God's goodness and delightful world each day. Let laughter take the form of praise.

• Gather humor from the creativity of your own family members. During family times together, occasionally ask such questions as these:

1. What is the funniest thing that has ever happened to you personally?

2. What was the most pleasurable thing you experienced today?

3. If you were alone on a desert island, what would you do to create delight and enjoyment?

4. If you were going to invent a cartoon strip, who would be your central character, and what would be the funniest trait of that character?

5. Who is the jolliest person in the family (include cousins, uncles, grandparents, etc.)? Why do you think so?)

6. Is a cucumber funny? What about a coconut? What do you think is the funniest fruit or vegetable? The funniest animal? Why?

7. How have you enjoyed God today?

Literature Cited

Barr, Browne. "The Bishop and the Banana Peel." *Christian Century*, (21–28 July 1976): 661–663.

Barth, Karl. *Dogmatics in Outline*. New York: Harper and Row, 1964.

Bayly, Joseph. *Out of My Mind*. Wheaton, IL: Tyndale House Publishers, 1970.

Bishop, Morris. *Saint Francis of Assisi*. Boston: Little, Brown, and Co., 1974.

Chapman, Antony and Hugh Foot, eds. *Humor and Laughter: Theory, Research and Applications*. New York: Wiley and Sons, 1976.

_____ . *It's a Funny Thing, Humour*. Oxford: Pergamon Press, 1977.

Cousins, Norman. *Anatomy of an Illness as Perceived by the Patient*. New York: Norton, 1979.

Cross, Farrell, and Wilbur Cross. "Laughter: A Way to Better Health." *Science Digest*, (November 1977): 16.

Ebert, Bruce. "The Healthy Family." *Family Therapy*, 5 (1978): 227–232.

Ellis, William. "Solve That Problem—With Humor." *Reader's Digest*, (May 1973): 189–192.

Flynn, Leslie B. *Serve Him With Mirth: The Place of Humor in the Christian Life*. Grand Rapids, MI: Zondervan Publishing House, 1960.

Freud, Sigmund. *Jokes and Their Relation to the Unconscious*. New York: W. W. Norton and Co., Inc., 1960. Originally published as *Der Witz und Seine Beziehung zum Unbewussten* (Leipzig and Vienna: Deuticke, 1905).

Fromme, Allan. "The Serious Side of Humor." *50 Plus*, (November 1980): 50–51.

Fry, W. F., Jr., and Melanie Allan. *Make 'em Laugh*. Palo Alto: Science and Behavior Books. 1975.

Getzels, J. W., and P. W. Jackson. *Creativity and Intelligence*. New York: Wiley and Sons, 1962.

107

Goldstein, Jeffrey, and Paul McGhee, eds. *The Psychology of Humor*. New York: Academic Press, 1972.

Greig, J. Y. T. *The Psychology of Laughter and Comedy*. London: George Allen and Unwin, 1923.

Grotjahn, Martin. *Beyond Laughter*. New York: McGraw Hill, 1957.

Hamilton, William. "Humor: Plausible and Demonic." *Christian Century*, (8 July 1959): 807.

Harper, John. "What Your Sense of Humor Reveals About You." *National Enquirer*, (2 December 1980).

Horstman, Judith. "No Joke: Humor Museum in Works." *USA Today*, (6 February 1984).

Hyers, Conrad, ed. *Holy Laughter*. New York: Seabury Press, 1969.

Hyers, Conrad. *Comic Vision and the Christian Faith*. New York: Pilgram Press, 1981.

Isaacs, Susan. "Family Laughter." *Parents*, (August 1983): 42–46.

Jungreis, Abigail. "Good For a Laugh." *Scholastic Update*, 116 (14 October 1983).

Kilby, Clyde S. *Christianity and Aesthetics*. Downers Grove, IL: Inter Varsity Press, 1961.

Knutson, Ted. "Read All About It! Newspapers Can Teach Kids." *Chicago Tribune*, (2 March 1984).

Koestler, Arthur. *The Act of Creation*. New York: Dell Publishing, 1964.

Leacock, S. B. *Humor: Its Theory and Technique*. New York: Dodd, Mead, Co., 1935.

Lewis, C. S. *Screwtape Letters*. New York: Macmillan Company, 1944.

Lobsenz, Norman. "The Joy of Family Rituals." *McCalls*, (December 1980): 8–12.

Lorenz, Konrad *On Aggression*. New York: Bantam, 1963.

Maslow, A. H. *Motivation and Human Behavior*, rev. ed. New York: Harper and Row, 1970.

McCarthy, Dennis. "Warning: Humor Could Be Hazardous to Your Illness." *The Saturday Evening Post*, (September 1983): 30–32.

McGhee, Paul. *Humor: Its Origin and Development*. San Francisco: W. H. Freeman, 1979.

McGinley, Phyllis. *The Province of the Heart*. New York: Viking Press, 1959.

McLuhan, Marshall. *The Medium is the Massage*. New York: Bantam Books, 1967.

Milofsky, David. "What Makes a Good Family?" *Redbook*, (August 1981): 58–62.

Mindess, Harvey. *Laughter and Liberation*. Los Angeles: Nash Publishing, 1971.

Moody, Raymond A., Jr. *Laugh After Laugh*. Jacksonville, FL: Headwaters Press, 1978.

Morreall, John. *Taking Laughter Seriously*. Albany: State University of New York Press, 1983.

Mullaly, Margaret Jane. "The Structure and Process of Humor Within Adult Sister Relationships." (Ph.D. diss., California School of Professional Psychology, Univ. of Calif., Berkeley, 1981).

O'Connell, W. E. "The Adaptive Functions of Wit and Humor." *Journal of Abnormal and Social Psychology*, (1960): 263–270.

Ogilvie, Lloyd John. *Let God Love You*. Waco, TX: Word Books, 1974.

Overstreet, Harry. *Influencing Human Behavior*. New York: W. W. Norton and Company, 1925.

Peter, Laurence J. "Today's Humor." *U. S. News and World Report*, (18 October 1982): 66.

Peter, Laurence J., and Bill Dana. *The Laughter Prescription*. New York: Random House, 1982.

Robinson, Vera. *Humor and the Health Professions*. Thorofare, N J: C. B. Slack, Inc., 1977.

Rogers, Carl. *Freedom to Learn*. Columbus, OH: Charles E. Merrill, 1969.

Schneyer, Bernice. "Mothering is a Ticklish Situation, or the Contributions of a Sense of Humor to Mothering." (Ph.D. diss., Union for Experimenting Colleges and Universities, 1981).

Talmage, Thomas, "Laughter in the Bible." *Biblical Research Monthly*, (September 1980): 14–15.

Trueblood, Elton. *The Humor of Christ.* New York: Harper and Row, 1964.

Vos, Nelvin. *For God's Sake Laugh!* Richmond, VA: John Knox Press, 1967.

Walsh, J. J. *Laughter and Health.* New York: Appleton, 1928.

Welliver, Dotsey. *I Need You Now, God, While the Grape Juice is Running All Over the Floor.* Winona Lake, IN: Light and Life Press, 1975.

Wilson, Glenn, John Rust, and Judith Kasriel. "Genetic and Family Origins of Humor Preferences: A Twin Study." *Psychological Reports,* 41 (October 1977: 659–660.